More than ENOUGH!

Activating God's Blessings in Your Life Today

DAVID CERULLO

**Activating God's Blessings
in Your Life Today**

by David Cerullo

© 2015 David Cerullo, Inspiration Ministries

ISBN: 978-1-936177-26-4

Published by:

INSPIRATION MINISTRIES
PO Box 7750
Charlotte, NC 28241

+1 803-578-1899

inspiration.org

Printed in the United States of America.

TABLE *of* CONTENTS

PART ONE: A Vision for a Better Life

PART TWO: Blessing Keys for Your Breakthrough

PART THREE: Living in the Land of More Than Enough

Part One:

A Vision
for a
Better Life

INTRODUCTION

Your Title Deed to a New Land

Imagine having a life where you never again need to worry about having enough money to pay your rent or mortgage...your utility bills, car payment, or medical bills. Your credit card debt is gone, and there are no more bill collectors calling to harass you.

In this new life of abundance, you not only have enough to meet the needs of your family, but you are so blessed by God that you also can help others who are in need. And you find great joy in generously supporting ministries that send the Good News of Jesus Christ to the nations of the world.

My friend, this is not just a distant dream—it is God's will for your life! Instead of remaining in the land of Not Enough or Barely Enough, your Heavenly Father wants you to live in His amazing land of More Than Enough.

This book is a roadmap to that land of abundance. It not only will give you a vision for the kind of life God wants you to have, but it also will give you powerful keys for how to *experience* that life today.

The Bible is a book of God's covenant promises. It's literally your **title deed** to the land of More Than Enough. But the title deed will do you no good unless you take steps of faith to *enter* and *possess* the Promised Land God has set before you.

Are you ready?

Testimonies of God's Faithfulness

The Bible is *filled* with stories of people who followed God's instructions and received a breakthrough in some area of their life. Some had been sick for many years, but they suddenly were healed. Others were in such dire poverty that their very survival was at stake, but God brought them miraculous abundance.

Many of the Bible's greatest heroes were *desperate for a miracle* at one time or another in their life. Does that describe *you* today? Do you feel like you've tried everything and looked everywhere? Does it seem like all hell has broken loose in your life and that it's impossible for things to change?

Know that God has a plan and a purpose for you—to give you a bright and hope-filled future (Jeremiah 29:11). The Biblical accounts of God's faithful provision to men and women who trusted Him are meant to encourage *your* steadfast confidence in Him today: *"Let us hold fast the confession of our hope without wavering, for He who promised is faithful"* (Hebrews 10:23).

Remember: The devil is not in control. Yes, Satan would love to send you stress, strife, poverty, depression, loneliness, anxiety, and sickness. But God's Word promises victory when we put our trust in Him: *"Thanks be to God who ALWAYS leads us in triumph in Christ"* (2 Cor-inthians 2:14).

You may be thinking, "It would take a *miracle* to set me free from my problems, David." Well, friend, that's exactly what God wants to give you!

What Breakthrough Do You Need?

Even if you have faced long-standing problems, the message in this book can be a "NOW" word for you, preparing you for the break-through you need. Hebrews 11:1 says, *"Now faith is the substance of things hoped for, the evidence of things not seen."* That's the kind of faith you and I need: *"NOW faith"*!

I don't believe you've picked up this book by accident. Even if you're looking for hope when it feels like all hope is gone, know that I've writ-ten these pages with YOU in mind!

What do you need from God today? He stands ready to give you...

- Answers to a desperate situation
- Freedom from poverty and debt
- His healing touch in your body
- Restoration of a broken relationship
- A more intimate relationship with Him

My prayer is that as you read through these pages, your heart will be completely open to the supernatural work only God can do. This is NOT a self-help book, telling you just to "try harder" or attempt to reinvent yourself in your own strength.

God wants you to turn to *Him* as your Source and Provider. He wants you to depend on *Him*, not on your job, your relationships, your bank account, your pastor, the government, or your own ingenuity.

The Lord also wants to free you from fear and worry, as Paul told the Philippians:

> *Don't worry about anything; instead, pray about everything. Tell God what you need, and thank him for all he has done. Then you will experience God's peace, which exceeds anything we can understand. His peace will guard your hearts and minds as you live in Christ Jesus* (Philippians 4:6-7 NLT).

So regardless of the anxious, painful, or difficult situation you may be facing today, know that your Heavenly Father loves you and wants you to trust Him and experience His peace and prosperity.

Psalm 35:27 says, *"Let the LORD be magnified, who has pleasure in the prosperity of His servant."* Isn't that beautiful? God takes PLEASURE in *your* PROSPERITY. Not only that, but He says in Deuteronomy 8:18 that He wants to give you the POWER to PROSPER and *"get wealth."*

What Land Are YOU in Today?

God doesn't want you or *any* of His children to suffer lack. So why should you keep living in the land of Not Enough or Barely Enough, when the Lord can bring you into His incredible land of MORE Than Enough?

Through the principles in this book, you can experience a life of overflowing abundance (Psalm 23:5), with more than enough of *everything*. That means more than enough energy...more than enough time...more than enough joy for living. And you also can have more than enough financial provision, enabling you to give to others out of the abundance He has given you.

Immediately after telling the Corinthians to sow bountifully in God's Kingdom, Paul provides this fantastic promise about the harvest they will receive for their faithfulness: *"God is able to make all grace abound toward you, that you, always having all sufficiency in all things, may have an abundance for every good work"* (2 Corinthians 9:8).

Take a moment to let these words sink in. Wouldn't you like to have *"all sufficiency in all things"*? Wouldn't it be wonderful to have *"an abundance for every good work"*?

You may want to take a look at some other translations as well. For example, the NLT says it this way: *"God will generously provide all you need. Then you will always have **everything you need** and **plenty left over** to share with others."*

No matter what your experience has been in the past, this is God's will for you as His beloved child. Because of His favor, you can have a life of overflowing abundance: *"...everything you need and plenty left over to share with others."*

In addition to giving you keys for a breakthrough from God, this book will help you discover something even more important: a lifestyle where God's *continuous* blessings are a way of life. Instead of merely experiencing a sporadic array of blessings, you will learn how to *abide* in Christ, confident of His constant presence and provision.

Sadly, too many Christians are experiencing a quality of life far below the blessings God intends for them. Often they are ignorant that health, prosperity, and emotional peace are their heritage as a Believer. Yet God's Word makes this clear: *"Beloved, I pray that you may **prosper in all things** and be in **health**, just as your soul prospers"* (3 John 1:2).

Notice the amazing scope of the prosperity God desires for you. His plan is not just to prosper you in *some* things, nor just *spiritual* things: He wants you to *"prosper in **ALL** things"*!

I've never been more convinced that God wants to transform your circumstances, your health, your relationships, your finances, and your emotions. He has a plan to get you unstuck and lead you into an amazing place of blessings—*"far more than you could ever imagine or guess or request in your wildest dreams!"* (Ephesians 3:20 MSG).

Thanks for joining me on this life-changing journey to a new level of blessings and breakthroughs in your life. Your new life can start *today*.

God bless you!

David

Chapter 1

STEPS TO OVERFLOWING ABUNDANCE

Throughout the pages of Scripture, God often showed Himself as a miraculous Provider when His people faced seemingly impossible situations. Perhaps you've heard the beautiful observation, "Our *extremity* is God's *opportunity!*"

Friend, if you are facing a difficult situation today, you're a prime candidate for a breakthrough from God. And there's a great story in Matthew 14:14-21 that will give you a glimpse of what it looks like to go from lack to abundance.

This passage begins with Jesus teaching and healing an enormous crowd of people. When evening came, the disciples told Jesus that He should send the multitudes away so they could get some food. They recognized it was a dangerous situation to have thousands of hungry people roaming the countryside.

However, Jesus shocked them by saying, *"They do not need to go away. You give them something to eat"* (v. 16).

Replying to Him, the disciples pointed out how ludicrous this was, *"We have here only five loaves and two fish"* (v. 17). In essence, they were saying, "Jesus, get serious. We are living in the land of Not Enough when it comes to feeding thousands of people. Five loaves and two fish are clearly not adequate to meet the enormous need."

Perhaps you are facing a situation much like this. You're surrounded by an overwhelming need, and the resources on hand are insufficient to even make a dent. So what can you do?

This is where the story begins to get really exciting—and practical as well. Instead of conceding that the circumstances were hopeless, Jesus pointed to the loaves and fish and told His bewildered followers, *"Bring them here to Me"* (v. 18).

You see, this is always the starting point of our miracle—when we take the resources in *our* hands and place them instead in *Jesus'* hands. At this point the loaves and fish suddenly became a SEED that Jesus took and multiplied. The Lord took their meager resources, looked up to Heaven, and blessed the loaves before breaking them and giving them back to the disciples.

Notice that Jesus gave the loaves and fish BACK to the disciples. Isn't that wonderful? The same resources they entrusted to the Lord were given back to them in the form of an abundant harvest—one that not only would meet their own needs, but also feed thousands of hungry people!

The disciples became part of the miracle as they freely distributed the loaves and fish to the crowd: *"So they all ate and were filled, and they took up twelve baskets full of the fragments that remained. Now those who had eaten were about five thousand men, besides women and children"* (vs. 20-21).

What a great crescendo to the story. At the beginning of the passage, the disciples were in the land of Not Enough. I'm sure they would have been thrilled if Jesus even gave them Barely Enough—avoiding a riot among the hungry crowd.

However, Jesus did much more than they could dream or imagine (Ephesians 3:20). They not only had *enough* to meet the need—they had **More Than Enough**, with 12 overflowing baskets of leftovers!

My friend, I encourage you to read this story one more time, asking God to show you what steps *you* may still need to take in order to receive your breakthrough. Don't worry if your resources seem totally inadequate to meet the needs around you. The key is to *bring everything to Jesus.* Trust Him with the seeds in your hand, and expect Him to multiply them into an overflowing harvest.

Where Are You Looking?

One of the keys to the loaves and fish miracle was that the disciples learned to *look to Jesus* instead of to their own resources. He is *"the author and finisher of our faith"* (Hebrews 12:2), and we will always be disappointed if we look to anyone or anything other than Him as our Source.

In some ways, the world's economic turmoil the past few years may actually be a blessing in disguise. Why? Because these difficult times are compelling many Believers to reassess whether they're truly trusting in the Lord as their Provider.

It's one thing to claim we're trusting in God for our provision when we have a good job, lots of equity in our home, and a growing 401(k) fund for our retirement. But what happens to our faith when the whole financial system is shaking and our resources seem to be drying up instead of growing?

Friend, it has never been more important for God's people to learn the secrets of coming to Him as *Jehovah-Jireh*—our faithful Provider—even when every human resource seems to be failing us.

Instead of trying to find hope in our circumstances, the Lord wants us to look to *Him* for overflowing abundance that has nothing to do with the economic systems of this world!

Heavenly Citizenship

If I asked you which country you're a citizen of, how would you respond? Perhaps you would say, "I'm a citizen of the United States" or "I live in the United Kingdom."

If I pressed a little further and asked how things were *going* in your country, you might say, "The economy is pretty sluggish right now, which is making life pretty hard for me."

However, consider this: The Bible says *"our citizenship is in **Heaven**"* (Philippians 3:20)! Heaven is a "country" where there's never been a recession or economic downturn. In Heaven there's no poverty or lack, nor is there any sickness or broken relationships. God's Heavenly Kingdom is like no country we've ever seen on earth, and there's never been a foreclosure or bankruptcy there!

But the fact is that most Christians in Western nations today are much too earthbound—wrapped up in this world instead of looking to God's Kingdom as their source of provision. We've forgotten the Bible's clear instruction: *"Set your mind on the things above, not on the things that are on earth"* (Colossians 3:2). As a result, we've put our hope in man's economy instead of God's.

Do you need a new beginning in your life today? Then you need to get a new perspective on where to look for your provision. The psalmist says this well:

> *Unto You I lift up my eyes,*
> *O You who dwell in the heavens.*
>
> *Behold, as the eyes of servants look to the hand of their masters,*
> *As the eyes of a maid to the hand of her mistress,*
> *So our eyes look to the LORD our God,*
> *Until He has mercy on us* (Psalm 123:1-2).

Heaven is the ultimate land of More Than Enough. And the more you set your heart on the Lord of Heaven, the more you will experience that kind of overflowing abundance and peace.

Chapter 2

YOUR JOURNEY TO A NEW LAND

The Christian life is a journey, as the psalmist beautifully described: *"Blessed is the man whose strength is in You, whose heart is set on pilgrimage...They go from strength to strength"* (Psalm 84:5-7).

Romans 12:2 tells us not to be conformed to this world, but to be *transformed* by the renewing of our mind. Paul also speaks of our transformation in 2 Corinthians 3:18, reminding us that as we gaze upon the glory of the Lord, we are increasingly *transformed* into that same image, from glory to glory.

Transformation speaks of change over time. This is good news, because you don't have to remain stuck in your present circumstances. As you set your heart toward God's best for your life, He can guide you on the right path and strengthen you for the journey.

The Israelites started out living in slavery in Egypt before journeying through the wilderness to the Promised Land. Their experience paints a helpful picture of three distinct "lands" people live in today regarding God's abundance. Whether you know it or not, *you* are living in one of these three lands too:

Egypt – THE LAND OF "NOT ENOUGH." When the children of Israel lived in Egypt, they were slaves to cruel taskmasters and given only meager rations of food (Exodus 1).

The Wilderness – THE LAND OF "BARELY ENOUGH." After being delivered from their bondage and scarce provisions in Egypt, the Israelites wandered for 40 years in the wilderness. Despite their failure to consistently trust and obey the Lord, He met all their needs in the wilderness. While He provided manna for them to eat each day, it couldn't be stored up, nor were there any leftovers (Exodus 16:14-21). During this stage of their journey, God's people were *surviving*, but not *thriving*.

Canaan – THE LAND OF "MORE THAN ENOUGH." The Israelites probably got used to their daily routine of gathering manna and having barely enough. But God had so much *more* planned for them in the Promised Land (Canaan). Scripture describes this as *"an exceedingly good land"* that had huge crops and *"flows with milk and honey"* (Numbers 14:7-8).

Which of these three lands are *you* living in today? Sadly, most Christians seem to be living in the land of Not Enough or Barely Enough. Their joy in life goes up and down with the daily stock market reports, or they're anxious every month about whether they'll even be able to make their mortgage or rent payment.

But this is not how God wants us to live! You don't have to die and go to Heaven to begin experiencing the land of More Than Enough!

Let me explain...

A New Economy

When the Israelites left the wilderness and passed over the Jordan River into the Promised Land, they were entering a whole new economy. Soon God's daily supply of manna stopped, and He began supplying their needs in a very different way. Instead of giving His people supernatural manna from Heaven, the Lord met their needs through the principle of seedtime and harvest!

Look at how Canaan is described:

*The LORD your God is bringing you into a **good land**....a land*
of wheat and barley, of vines and fig trees and pomegranates,
*a land of olive oil and honey; a land where you will eat **food***
without scarcity**, in which **you will not lack anything
(Deuteronomy 8:7-9).

God was bringing them into a land of overflowing abundance, but in order to experience ongoing crops of wheat, barley, grapes, figs, pomegranates, and olives, they had to *plant* something...they had to *sow seeds*!

Often when I hear a Christian complaining that God hasn't met their needs, I ask, "Tell me what seeds you've planted." Puzzled by my question, the person often responds, "Dave, what does *that* have to do with the Lord meeting my needs?"

Dear friend, that has *everything* to do with God's provision in your life! He wants to bring you from the *old* economy—the sparse provisions of the "wilderness" and the unreliable financial systems of this earth—into the abundant, faithful economy of His Kingdom!

What Are You Waiting For?

Many people are waiting for their harvest from God, but there's just one problem: They haven't yet planted any seeds!

What kind of farmer would operate like that? In the natural realm, a farmer knows his harvest will never be any greater than the seeds he's planted in faith, usually months earlier.

God wants you to live in the land of More Than Enough, but you've got to quit waiting for the manna to drop from the sky! Yes, God's supernatural provision will come, but it will come after you faithfully continue to plant seeds by faith into the good ground of His Kingdom.

Perhaps the breakthrough you need from God today isn't financial provision, but rather healing for your body, restoration of your relationship with a loved one, or simply greater peace in your heart. The good news is that God can take the financial seeds you plant and transform them into *whatever* harvest you need!

Trust God today—with your time, talent, and treasure. He can bring you from Egypt's bondage or the scarcity of the wilderness into a whole new economy—the land of More Than Enough!

Chapter 3

ARE YOU READY TO BE BLESSED?

Does God want to bless you with prosperity and abundance? Of course He does! What father would want his children to live in poverty and suffer lack? The pages of Scripture are full of references to God as your loving Heavenly Father who wants to give you His best—everything you could ever need.

If you are willing to *"ask," "seek,"* and *"knock,"* Jesus promises that your Father will gladly respond:

> *Ask, and it will be given to you; seek, and you will find; knock, and it will be opened to you. For everyone who asks receives, and he who seeks finds, and to him who knocks it will be opened.*
>
> *Or what man is there among you who, if his son asks for bread, will give him a stone? Or if he asks for a fish, will he give him a serpent? If you then, being evil, know how to give good gifts to your children, how much more will your Father who is in heaven give good things to those who ask Him!* (Matthew 7:7-11).

There are *hundreds* of similar Biblical promises about God's desire to bless and prosper His children when we walk in a covenant relationship with Him. Yet a fierce battle is raging today over the Bible's teachings about prosperity. Many well-meaning Christians have accepted the lie that God takes pleasure in giving them hardships and financial lack instead of blessing and abundance.

How sad this is! When told about God's desire to bless and prosper them, these misinformed folks say, "I believe that God chooses some people to abound and others to suffer lack—so none of us has a right to *expect* His blessings." Humble as that may sound, it is completely contrary to the teachings of God's Word!

Prospering in ALL Things

Today there's lots of confusion about God's desire to bless us with prosperity and abundance, and much of this stems from a failure to properly understand the Biblical perspective. Critics often wrongly assume that advocates of the "prosperity message" are focused only on *material* blessings. "It's all about believing God for a big house or a Mercedes," they complain.

However, although God's prosperity certainly *includes* financial blessings, that's only a small part of what the abundant life is all about. In addition to providing His children with material abundance, the Lord *also* wants to bless us with good health...strong relationships...peace of mind...victory over addictions...and an intimate relationship with Him.

God wants to bless us in every possible way: in our spirit, soul, and body...in our finances, marriages, children, health, and spiritual lives. The Apostle John describes this kind of all-inclusive prosperity like this:

Beloved, I pray that you may prosper in all things and be in health, just as your soul prospers (3 John 1:2).

Do you see the amazing scope of the prosperity God desires for His children? His plan is not just to prosper us in some things, or just spiritual things: He wants us to *"prosper in **ALL** things"*!

This lines up perfectly with the powerful Hebrew and Greek words used in the Bible to describe God's blessings:

Blessing (Hebrew *barak*) – "To bestow good upon." This word is used a remarkable 330 times in the Bible!

Peace (Hebrew *shalom*) – "To be made whole, healthy, happy, prosperous, and at peace." This is another Hebrew word used throughout the Old Testament, 250 times in all!

Salvation (Greek *sozo*) – "To be saved, delivered, healed, restored, or kept safe." Like the Hebrew word *shalom*, the Greek word *sozo* speaks of God's desire not only to give us salvation in Heaven when we die, but also to bring restoration to every area of our lives today.

Prosper (Greek *euodoō*) – "To help on one's way, act wisely, and be successful and wealthy." Biblical prosperity stems from receiving God's wisdom and obeying His instructions on your journey. He promises that when you meditate on His Word and obey it, *"you will make your way prosperous, and then you will have good success"* (Joshua 1:8).

Based on these potent words describing the majestic scope of God's prosperity, it's clear that the abundant life (John 10:10) includes much more than material wealth. If critics would recognize the *totality* of God's desire to bless us, it would be much more difficult for them to reject the prosperity message as being unbalanced, self-serving, or materialistic.

The prosperity message is actually just an extension of what the Bible says about the loving nature of our Heavenly Father. One of His core traits is that He's a GIVER, as we're told in John 3:16 and a multitude of other verses.

Restoring What Adam Lost

The first thing God did after creating Adam and Eve was to BLESS them (Genesis 1:27-38). There were so many other ways He could have begun His relationship with humankind, but He chose to bless them, placing them in a beautiful garden where they had no lack.

Adam and Eve were placed in the land of More Than Enough, and that continues to be God's intention for His people. But instead of such a life, many Believers are living in the land of Barely Enough or Not Enough. Because of ignorance, unbelief, or disobedience, they forfeit God's intended blessings and live below their inheritance in Christ.

If you've been continually living with Barely Enough or Not Enough, I have good news for you today: Your Heavenly Father loves you, and He wants to bring you into a land of *overflowing abundance*. He wants to overwhelmingly bless you, so you can, in turn, be a great blessing to others.

What does it look like to go from lack to abundance? As we saw in Matthew 14:14-21, the disciples had Not Enough to feed the thousands of hungry people who had come to hear Jesus teach. But after they brought their five loaves and two fish to Jesus, a miracle happened: Everyone had plenty to eat, and they ended up with 12 full baskets of *leftovers*!

Within mere moments, Jesus' disciples went from a place of lack to an amazing experience of More Than Enough. And the same can happen for *you*...if you put your life and your resources into the hands of Jesus.

Believe and You Will Receive!

If you don't *believe* in God's prosperity, it's unlikely you will *receive* His prosperity. Why? Because faith is an indispensable key to activating and receiving the promises of God.

Jesus said, *"It shall be done to you according to your faith"* (Matthew 9:29). What an incredible principle! If you believe God will prosper you, He will. But if you don't believe He will prosper you, He won't! You see, God will honor your *faith*.

The story is told of a man during the Great Depression who lost his job and became homeless. Living on a street corner, he begged every day from those who passed by, hoping for enough spare change to buy a meal.

One day a wealthy man passed by and had compassion on the homeless man. He stopped and wrote a large check, telling the man, "Here, this will help."

However, the homeless man looked at the check in disbelief, unable to believe that a total stranger would give him so much money. He put the check in his pocket and continued to beg.

My friend, like the homeless man in this story, in Christ you've become richer than you can even imagine. You don't have to keep begging, looking to the government or other people to meet your needs. God's Word says He's given you a huge check—with *your* name on it!

I pray today that you will see God's amazing love for you. In the chapters ahead, I'll share powerful keys for how your life can overflow with such abundance that countless others will be impacted, both in this life and in eternity.

Chapter 4

RELEASE HEAVEN'S BOUNTY

Genesis 28 tells the intriguing story of a spectacular dream Jacob had one night in a barren place, far from his home: *"He dreamed, and behold, a ladder was set up on the earth, and its top reached to heaven; and there the angels of God were ascending and descending on it"* (v. 12).

I'm sure this dream got Jacob's attention right away. But what did it mean? First of all, the ladder between Heaven and earth showed Jacob this powerful and life-changing truth:

The resources of Heaven are a lot closer than we think!

Too often, Believers view Heaven as some distant and inaccessible place, with no impact on our lives until after we die. But Jacob's dream showed him there is constant activity taking place between Heaven and earth! Because of that, amazing miracles are possible *right now*, including financial breakthroughs, physical healings, and restored relationships.

After Jacob witnessed this startling interaction between Heaven and earth, the Lord promised to give him that land and said, *"In you and in your descendants shall all the families of the earth be blessed"* (v. 14).

Jacob's encounter with the Lord impacted him so greatly that he declared the spot to be a special sanctuary of God's presence:

> Surely the LORD is in this place, and I did not know it...How awesome is this place! This is none other than the house of God, and this is the gate of heaven (vs. 16-17).

In the physical realm, this piece of ground was just a desolate section of desert. But Jacob dedicated it as a special place...the very gate of Heaven!

My friend, this is God's purpose for your life as well! He wants to bless you and make you a blessing (Genesis 12:2)—not only for your descendants, but also to bless the nations with the Gospel of Jesus Christ!

Perhaps this seems like an impossible mission, but God promises to be with you all along the way, just as He promised Jacob: *"I will not leave you until I have done what I have promised you"* (Genesis 28:15). God will be faithful to complete the work He's started in you (Philippians 1:6)!

Opening the Gate for Others

What was true for Jacob is also true for us today. God desires to open *"the gate of heaven"* in our lives in order to pour out His blessings...provision...healing...deliverance...guidance...breakthroughs...joy—and whatever else we may need!

As we draw near to Him *"in the secret place"* (Psalm 91:1), the Lord wants to touch our lives with Heaven's supernatural bounty and healing power. No wonder the Bible promises that *"those who seek the LORD shall not lack ANY good thing"* (Psalm 34:10).

And once we experience the amazing resources God pours out through His Heavenly gateway, we respond by sending out His hope, healing, and salvation to a lost and needy world. Because God's love moves on our hearts, we want to *share* His blessings to help and impact others.

Jesus said to ask the Father for an ever-increasing measure of His Heavenly Kingdom to be unveiled through our lives on earth: *"Your kingdom come. Your will be done on earth as it is in heaven"* (Matthew 6:10). Is there great abundance in Heaven? Absolutely! But God wants to use *us* to release some of that abundance to meet needs on earth.

Remember: The "More Than Enough" message is not just about your personal comfort or luxury—it's about manifesting the blessings and abundance of Heaven to be a blessing to others. In Heaven there is no poverty, sickness, sin, or strife, and we should *"seek first"* that same Heavenly lifestyle, both for ourselves and for whatever circle of influence God gives us (Matthew 6:33).

The Kingdom Is at Hand!

Jesus didn't just talk about or preach about the Kingdom of Heaven— He *demonstrated* it! Rather than a faraway place that is only relevant after we die, Jesus described the Heavenly Kingdom as being *"at hand"* (Matthew 4:17):

- Do you need a financial breakthrough?
  Heaven's bounty is at hand!
- Do you need God's touch in your body?
  Heaven's healing power is at hand!
- Do you need victory over addiction or oppression from the enemy?
  Heaven's army is at hand to triumph over the powers of darkness!

The resources of Heaven are near you today, and they are More Than Enough to meet every need in your life. To receive them, all you have to do is reach out in faith:

The righteousness of faith speaks in this way, "Do not say in your heart, 'Who will ascend into heaven?'" (that is, to bring Christ down from above) or, "Who will descend into the abyss?'" (that is, to bring Christ up from the dead). But what does it say? **"The word is near you, in your mouth and in your heart"** *(Romans 10:6-8).*

God wants to bless you through His Heavenly portals, enabling you to help fill the earth with the knowledge of His glory as the waters cover the sea (Habakkuk 2:14). Souls in eternity will be grateful the Lord blessed *you* with overflowing abundance!

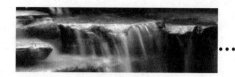

Chapter 5

MOVE FROM POVERTY TO PROVISION

Many people today are in a deep financial pit. Debts have piled up, and they find themselves needing a huge financial miracle from God. Often the situation looks hopeless, and it's hard to believe that a new beginning is possible.

If you find yourself in a situation like this, there's a good chance you've been living in the land of Not Enough or Barely Enough for quite a while. You might even have the zip code or postal code memorized by now!

Second Kings chapter four tells the amazing story of a widow who found herself in a dire predicament, with no apparent way out. With her husband gone, it was hard to make ends meet. The situation had gotten so bad that she told the prophet Elisha, *"The creditor is coming to take my two sons to be his slaves"* (2 Kings 4:1).

At first it might be hard for us to relate to this statement. A creditor taking people into slavery? Yet that is exactly what happens when we are in debt. God warns us in Proverbs 22:7 that *"the borrower becomes the lender's slave."* While this may seem like harsh language, many of you have already experienced this terrible slavery in your own lives.

Financial slavery is not God's will for you! He has called you to be one of His beloved sons or daughters, and His kids aren't meant to be slaves of *anyone*!

However, perhaps you are like so many people today, needing a financial breakthrough to end your bondage to poverty and lack. If so, help is on the way! The Lord has a word of instruction for *you* today, just as He had for this poor woman.

What Do You Already Have?

Elisha's response to the widow's cry for help may seem puzzling at first. *"Tell me,"* he asks her, **"what do you have in the house?"** (v. 2). Instead of offering to give her something from his own resources, he first inquires about the resources she already has.

"What do you *have*?!" That is God's question to *us* as well. He never asks us for something we *don't* have, but He rightfully expects us to surrender everything we *do* have to Him. Yet how can someone who is on the verge of financial ruin be expected to surrender even the little bit that they still have? It is here that the story starts getting exciting.

The widow clearly doesn't like Elisha's question. *"Your maidservant has **nothing** in the house **but** a jar of oil,"* she replies (v. 2). While her first thought was that she had *"nothing,"* she remembered a *"but"*—a jar of oil.

Perhaps you are in exactly that circumstance today. You feel as though you have *nothing*. And even if you have some trivial-seeming resources, they appear to be *worthless* in the face of the extreme financial need you are facing.

However, Elisha saw the situation much differently: The widow's small jar of oil could become a seed to bring prosperity she never dreamed possible!

Triggering Your Miracle

Then Elisha gave the widow some rather peculiar advice: *"Go, borrow vessels from everywhere, from all your neighbors—empty vessels; do not gather just a few. And when you have come in, you shall shut the door behind you and your sons; then pour it into all those vessels, and set aside the full ones"* (vs. 3-4).

Why would the widow need **empty vessels** when she seemingly had nothing to put in them? The neighbors probably thought she was getting a little wacky at this point! She was preparing for a miracle, even when none seemed possible. Perhaps you have received this same response from people around you when you tell them your breakthrough is at hand!

Elisha went on to tell her to *"shut the door"* behind her. Friend, there is a time when we need to enter into the presence of God and shut the door behind us. We need to shut the door on the devil. We need to shut the door on our naysaying neighbors. We need to shut the door to *anything* that would keep us from our new beginning of God's favor in our life.

Notice that the miracle doesn't begin until the widow starts to **pour out** what she has. If we give, the Bible says, we will receive back an abundant, overflowing return (Luke 6:38). This woman learned to sacrificially sow a seed out of her *lack*, and this became the key to her abundant prosperity.

Within a very short period of time, this impoverished widow went from financial ruin to a plentiful supply. Not only was her debt paid off, but she and her sons also had more than enough to live on. Elisha told her, *"Go, sell the oil and pay your debt; and you and your sons live on the rest"* (v. 7). Her scarcity was reversed when she obediently poured out what she had.

Sometimes it's easy to think that your situation is so bleak that, at best, it will surely take a long time to dig out of the pit you are in. And sometimes it does.

But the story of this distressed widow shows that incredible things can happen when you obey God's instructions: His favor can suddenly transform your situation from poverty to provision. In mere moments, you can find yourself transported from the land of Not Enough to the land of More Than Enough!

Chapter 6

GO FROM FRUSTRATION TO FRUITFULNESS

I'm sure some of you who are reading this book are still wary of believing that God can bring you into the land of More Than Enough. Perhaps you've spent years, or even decades, in the lands of Not Enough or Barely Enough, and it's really hard to imagine things getting any better.

Let me tell you a story that may help...

In Luke 5, Jesus had been sitting in Simon Peter's fishing boat in order to teach the huge crowds that gathered around Him at the Lake of Gennesaret. When He finished His teaching, He told Peter, *"Launch out into the deep and let down your nets for a catch"* (v. 4).

There's an important message of encouragement for *you* in this word of instruction: The Lord wants to take you DEEPER and He wants you to reap a great HARVEST. But notice that Peter needed to *reposition himself* in order to receive the intended breakthrough. If he had insisted on just staying put, He would have missed out on the amazing blessing that was in store for him.

At first Peter protested, saying, *"Master, we have toiled all night and caught nothing..."* (v. 5). Perhaps you can relate to Peter's frustration.

You've tried so hard to make ends meet, but nothing has seemed to work. Maybe you've sent out numerous resumes in pursuit of a new job, but like Peter, you've *"caught nothing."*

Friend, God understands your frustration today. He knows how hard you've tried. But He also knows that your breakthrough won't come through your own strength, but because of His divine favor and intervention.

Despite his frustration over past failures and disappointments, Peter decided to obey Jesus' instruction: *"...nevertheless at Your word I will let down the net."*

Peter's step of faith and obedience turned out to be a pivotal moment, transforming not just the outcome of that day, but his entire life after that: *"When they had done this, they caught a great number of fish, and their net was breaking"* (v. 6).

What a dramatic turnaround! The story had begun with Peter and his fishing partners living in the land of Not Enough, but now they suddenly found themselves in the land of More Than Enough! And this remarkable turn of events all happened because they dared to believe Jesus' instruction and *"launch out"* into deeper waters.

These fishermen had no doubt seen a variety of catches over the years, but *nothing* like this. They were *"astonished at the catch of fish which they had taken"* (v. 9).

Friend, I believe this is God's message for YOU today: You haven't seen *anything* yet! He wants to bless you so abundantly that it far surpasses any blessing you've experienced in the past. Just as the boats suddenly overflowed with fish, your life is destined to overflow with God's blessings when you heed His instructions!

This story ends with a beautiful statement that is often overlooked: *"They forsook all and followed Him"* (v. 11). Why were Peter and his comrades able to take such a bold step of faith to abandon their fishing boats and careers? *Because they had seen Jesus' ability to provide for them when they obeyed Him!*

A Refresher Course

Peter and his friends had seen a stunning demonstration of what it means to go from the land of Not Enough to the land of More Than Enough. Their faith was stirred to put their full reliance on Jesus to meet their future needs, and they wholeheartedly followed Him.

Have you ever seen God do a miracle in your life? It may have been a financial breakthrough...a physical healing...the calming of your emotions...or the restoration of a broken relationship. When you saw the power of God at work on your behalf, you determined that you would put your trust in Him for the rest of your life.

But if you're anything like me, you might need a reminder from time to time. Although you've seen God's breakthroughs in the past, you sometimes need a refresher course in what it means to trust Him.

In John 21, Peter and some of the other disciples were given this kind of refresher course in the steps toward overflowing abundance. Once again, they were out fishing. And again, they fished all night but caught nothing.

This time Jesus was on the shore, and He pointedly asked them whether they had any food. *"No,"* they told Him (v. 5). It's as if they had again found themselves in the land of Not Enough or Barely Enough—failing to experience the favor and blessing of God because they were living life on their own terms and in their own strength.

If that's where *you* find yourself today, don't despair. Listen for the Lord's word of instruction, and set your heart to DO what He tells you to do.

In this case, Jesus tells the men, *"Cast the net on the right side of the boat, and you will find some"* (v. 6). And again, the result was immediate and immense: *"Now they were not able to draw it in because of the multitude of fish."*

In mere moments, the disciples were right back in the land of More

Than Enough. The same can happen today for you, my friend. Listen for God's instructions, do what He says, and then get ready for your breakthrough!

Chapter 7

WHAT'S THE CATCH?

When you read about this message of More Than Enough, you may understandably be skeptical. "David, this sounds too good to be true," you may say to me. "There's got to be a catch somewhere."

Well, actually there *is* a catch in some ways. But the Bible is very straightforward about what it is: *If you want God to release the amazing abundance in **His** hands, then you first must release whatever resources you're holding in **your** hands.*

Your resources may not look like much right now, but that's not important. God will bless whatever you give Him...but you must give Him what He asks for!

The Scriptures are full of stories about the Lord asking people to give Him something He could transform or multiply. Here are just a few examples:

Abraham was asked to put his son Isaac on the altar (Genesis 22:1-18). As a result of his obedience, the Lord revealed Himself to Abraham as *Yahweh Yireh (Jehovah-Jireh)*, *"The-LORD-Will-Provide"* (v. 14), and promised: *"In your seed all the nations of the earth shall be blessed"* (v. 18).

Moses was asked to lay down his shepherd's rod (Exodus 4:1-5). After this event, the simple piece of wood was transformed into *"the rod of God"* (Exodus 4:20). Moses used it to bring God's judgment on the Egyptians (Exodus 9:23, 10:13), part the Red Sea (Exodus 14:16), bring gushing water out of a rock (Exodus 17:5-6), and defeat enemy armies (Exodus 17:8-13).

A boy was asked to give up his five loaves of bread and two fish (John 6:5-13). How many people could have been fed by these meager resources under normal circumstances? One or two? Maybe three? But when this boy's small supply of food was placed in Jesus' hands and blessed by Him, *thousands* of hungry people were fed! Even more remarkable, the disciples were able to gather up 12 full baskets of *leftovers*. What a testimony to the kind of overflowing abundance God intends for His people!

Although I could point to a lot more stories like this in God's Word, I hope you already get the point. The Lord will do amazing things with the resources you entrust into His hands—and this is your indispensable key to live in the land of More Than Enough.

Does It *Always* Work?

Perhaps you're thinking, "David, these are great stories, but are you saying these Biblical principles will ALWAYS work, bringing any Christian into a life of abundance?"

When someone asks me this important question, I usually respond: "Yes, the prosperity principles in God's Word ALWAYS work—but we have to *work* them!" In other words, there's nothing unreliable about the Lord's principles...the only question is whether or not we've *applied* the principles and obeyed His conditions.

If we are faithful and obedient to Him, it's up to God to fulfill the terms of His Word. We don't have to doubt Him on this, for His Word promises: *"God is not a man, that He should lie"* (Numbers 23:19).

The Lord will do *His* part, that's for sure. Our role is simply to meet

His conditions and then stand in faith: *"Having done all, to stand"* (Ephesians 6:13).

When our faith is tested, we must not give up or lose hope. We must keep believing, keep declaring God's Word, and keep exercising our faith. We also must wait *patiently*, realizing that some prayers may take many years before they come to pass.

We faced this kind of test when our son Ben strayed from the Lord for several years. Barbara and I would go into his empty room to pray, claim God's promises, and ask Him for a breakthrough.

At first, it seemed like nothing was happening. In fact, Ben's circumstances got even worse. But as we continued to align our prayers with specific promises in Scripture, the Holy Spirit moved on Ben's heart. He's now a powerful man of God who takes the Gospel of Jesus Christ to the nations!

Maintaining Your Expectancy

One of my primary purposes in writing this book is to build your faith to expect God's supernatural blessings throughout your life. I'm not referring to mere wishful thinking but to a patient, steadfast expectation grounded in God's unchanging Word.

But let's be honest: The Lord isn't bound by our timetable. Just as a farmer who has faithfully planted seeds can be confident he will reap *"in due time"* (Galatians 6:9), we must maintain our expectancy, even if our harvest takes more time than we expected.

My dad taught me many years ago always to look for parallels between the natural realm and the spiritual world, because God uses the natural to teach us about the spiritual (1 Corinthians 15:46).

This is so true concerning the parallels between a farmer's harvest of crops and *our* harvest of blessings after we've planted seeds into God's Kingdom.

In the natural realm, we plant seeds in our garden for a desired result, and then we invest time in turning the soil, adding nutrients, making sure the seeds are at the right depth, watering the ground, and pulling out weeds. After we've done all this, we wait expectantly for our harvest of fruit and vegetables.

The same kinds of steps are also necessary in the spiritual realm. Just as farmers invest their time, effort, and resources with an expectation of harvest, so should we have a desired result in mind as we sow spiritual seeds. And though we may not reap our spiritual harvest for some time, we must maintain a sense of expectancy, confident of God's faithfulness.

Not "Jack and the Beanstalk"

Many people think God's principles of abundance are like the "magic seeds" in the "Jack and the Beanstalk" story. According to that famous fairy tale, Jack's special seeds sprung up overnight, creating a huge beanstalk reaching far into the sky.

But *real* seeds don't work that way. No one goes out to plant seeds in their garden and then returns the next day to gather a bouquet of flowers or pick enough vegetables to make a salad. Nor can you expect a fully-formed apple tree to emerge the day you plant an apple seed in the ground.

Just as it takes *time* to reap a harvest in nature, the same is true of our spiritual seeds. We must be willing to wait long enough for our spiritual seeds to produce the harvests we desire.

Waiting reveals our obedience and our trust in the Lord's timing. While we're waiting, we must *water* and *nourish* our precious seeds with love and worship, obedience to God's Word, and an attitude of belief, expectancy, and thanksgiving.

No one said this is easy. We live in an "instant" world of fast foods, microwave ovens, immediate gratification, and "get rich quick" schemes. However, God's Kingdom is not like that. His principle of seedtime and harvest will *surely* bring you prosperity if you utilize it, but your harvest of blessings will come *"in due season."* In the meantime, *"Let us not grow weary in doing good"* (Galatians 6:9).

Prosperity Is a Process

Do you want to prosper in a certain area of your life? Then patiently sow your seeds in faith, realizing that prosperity is not an *event* but a *process.* Jesus describes this in Mark 4:28: *"The soil produces crops by itself; **first** the blade, **then** the head, **then** the mature grain in the head."*

If you've planted seeds in God's Kingdom, your harvest WILL come. It may not come in a dramatic windfall—one fell swoop—but it will *certainly* come in God's perfect time. If you've done your part, you can be confident His "prosperity process" will meet your every need (Philippians 4:10-19).

I know the waiting process can be difficult, but that's why the Lord encourages us with great promises like these in His Word:

> *Nor has the eye seen any God besides You,*
> ***Who acts for the one who waits for Him*** (Isaiah 64:4).

> *Those who **wait** on the LORD*
> *Shall renew their strength;*
> *They shall mount up with wings like eagles,*
> *They shall run and not be weary,*
> *They shall walk and not faint* (Isaiah 40:31).

> *"The Lord is good to those who **wait** for Him, to the person who seeks Him"* (Lamentations 3:25 NASB).

You can be confident your harvest is on the way—and it's worth waiting for!

Part Two:

BLESSING KEYS FOR YOUR BREAKTHROUGH

Chapter 8

Blessing Key: *One*

You're Blessed to Be a Blessing

My wife Barbara and I have received literally thousands of prayer requests from people struggling with painful situations. They've lost their jobs and lost their homes. Marriages are crumbling, and children are rebelling. Others are struggling to overcome addiction, or they're overwhelmed by depression. Their bodies are aching, and their spirits are deflated.

Many of those who write to us are longing for the Lord to move in their life, but they feel hopeless. They desperately need a breakthrough, but often they doubt God's love and His desire to intervene in their difficult circumstances.

As Barbara and I pray over needs like these, we feel people's pain. We know God *wants* to break through in their circumstances. He *wants* to do miracles in their lives. He *wants* to heal them. He *wants* to give them His joy and abundant provision. Our Heavenly Father's heart is *always* to bless His children.

Just as *our* hearts break when we encounter children of God who are dealing with dire situations, we know that *God's* heart breaks as well.

Since His Word clearly declares His desire to bless His children, what key could they be missing? What could possibly be blocking them from entering God's land of More Than Enough?

Through the years, Barbara and I have experienced some painful and challenging times of our own. Our faith has been tested by attacks on our health, our finances, our emotions, or our relationships. During these times, we knew we needed a miracle, but we sure couldn't see a miracle coming.

I can remember as if it were yesterday when we broke open our son's piggy bank just so we could go get a burger to split for our dinner. I was out of work, and we were broke. I didn't know how I was going to pay the car loan, make the mortgage payment, or put food on the table.

It's a terrible thing to feel like you can't provide for your family. I had a wife and a baby, and I was desperate. But God came through for us in a mighty and powerful way: He blessed me with a consulting job that paid thousands of dollars for a day's work, and then I in turn was able to bless my family and others as I gave out of what He had given me.

Know today that God wants to move in powerful ways to overcome the circumstances of *your* life. He is the Creator of the entire universe, and He has promised to bless you with new beginnings as you turn to Him in faith.

God's Covenant Blessings for *YOU*

Did you know that part of your calling as a Believer is to inherit the blessings of God? That's exactly what you're promised in 1 Peter 3:9: *"Knowing that you were called to this, that you may inherit a blessing."* When you consider how infinitely wealthy your Heavenly Father is, you can hardly imagine the amazing inheritance this is meant to be.

And I love God's promise in Genesis 12:2: *"I will bless you...and you shall be a blessing."* Stop for a minute and get a hold of this truth: God is saying to **YOU**, *"I will bless **YOU**...and **YOU** shall be a blessing."*

Now perhaps you're thinking, "Wait a minute, Dave. I know that Bible story, and God was talking to Abraham—not *me*—when He promised that."

Well, that's true. But according to Galatians 3, the promises God made to Abraham, He also made to *us*. This Scripture passage says that Abraham...

> ...believed God, and it was accounted to him for righteousness. Therefore know that only those who are of faith are sons of Abraham...that the blessing of Abraham might come upon the Gentiles in Christ Jesus, that we might receive the promise of the Spirit through faith...Now to Abraham and his Seed were the promises made (vs. 6–16).

Do you see what this says? Abraham's promises are *our* promises. If you're a Believer today...if Jesus Christ is your Lord and Savior...then you, too, are Abraham's seed, and the blessings and promises of Abraham are *yours*. And like Abraham, as you receive God's blessings, you can *be* a blessing to others!

The promise that God made to Abraham—and to you—was a **covenant.** God made this covenant in order to have a *relationship* with Abraham. Let me give you a great example to help you understand the concept of living in a covenant relationship with God.

On our wedding day, Barbara and I exchanged vows. We made promises to each other to love and cherish one another for the rest of our lives. Ours was a love relationship sealed by the covenant we made before God and all our wedding guests.

This is the kind of love relationship the Lord wants to have with you. He loves you so much that He wants you to live in a covenant relationship with Him *forever*.

A covenant is a solemn, binding agreement between two parties. To covenant with someone means that those involved will stand behind their word, no matter what. Just as Barbara and I made a covenant promise to be faithful to one another as husband and wife until we die, God has made promises to you as His child and covenant partner.

Friend, I urge you to grab hold of this powerful truth deep in your heart: **God is a God of covenants, and He is faithful to His covenant promises.** He can't and won't forget the promises He has made. He will stand behind His Word *every* time, and He will *never* be unfaithful to what He has covenanted with us to do.

The Lord is stirring such compassion in my heart for you right now. You *want* to believe this truth is for you. You *want* to believe it's this simple. You *want* to trust that God's covenant promises in the Bible can change your circumstances today.

But perhaps you're afraid. Maybe you've been waiting a long time for God to pour out His blessings in your life, and now you're discouraged, tired of waiting.

If this describes where you are today, then know that God understands. He sees your heart. He knows your need. He has compassion on your brokenness and discouragement, and He wants you to learn to trust Him.

You're not reading this book today by accident! In the midst of your difficult circumstances, God wants to break through and release His covenant blessings—not only to bless you, but also to equip you to be a blessing to others.

Don't let past disappointments cause you to turn away from your God-given destiny, your calling in Christ, your mission in life. Today can be the beginning of a breakthrough in your life.

Will Jesus Pass You By?

If you feel like God has passed you by, it's time for a new perspective. The Lord wants to intervene in *everyone's* circumstances. He is willing and ready to release His breakthroughs over *all* who have prepared their hearts to receive His best in their lives.

So what's missing? Well, the sad truth is that not everyone prepares their hearts for the Lord to bless them. As a result, many of God's children aren't walking in the reality of His covenant blessings that they so desperately need.

Let me tell you a story from the Bible to encourage you to prepare your heart to receive all God has planned for you…

One stormy and windy night, Jesus' disciples were in a boat out on the sea. They were weary from straining to row the boat to shore, and their situation was bleak. Mark 6:48 (NASB) says Jesus *"came to them, walking on the sea; and He intended to pass by them."* The disciples cried out in fear, thinking they were seeing a ghost.

But this story has such a great ending. When the disciples finally recognized Jesus, He assured them, *"Take courage; it is I. Do not be afraid"* (v. 50). Then He climbed into the boat with them, and the wind stopped.

My friend, this is precisely what Jesus wants to do in *your* life today. He wants to get into your "boat" with you—right there in the midst of your storms and difficult circumstances. He wants to speak a powerful word over your troubling situations, stilling the winds of adversity that the enemy has brought your way.

Yes, the devil will do everything he can to thwart God's plan for your health, your relationships, your emotions, and your finances. That's his agenda, for Jesus warns us in John 10:10 (NASB) that *"the thief comes only to steal and kill and destroy."*

But Jesus goes on to say, *"I came that they may have life, and have it abundantly."* You see, Satan doesn't have to get the last word on what happens to you. Jesus has come to give you an abundant life! Whatever you are going through right now, He wants to climb into your boat *today* and begin to turn things around.

Your Heavenly Father loves you. He is able and willing to intervene as you prepare your heart to receive His covenant blessings in your life.

If you're doubting whether God has a covenant blessing that fits your specific situation, look at Paul's words in Ephesians 1:3: *"Blessed be the God and Father of our Lord Jesus Christ, who has blessed us with **every spiritual blessing** in the heavenly places in Christ."* Notice how all-inclusive this promise is. God doesn't just want to provide you with SOME spiritual blessings, but rather He offers to give you EVERY spiritual blessing through your relationship with Christ.

And you are given a similar promise in Romans 8:32: *"He who did not spare His own Son, but delivered Him up for us all, how shall He not with Him also freely give us **all things**?"*

Isn't that fantastic? God has already given us the most precious gift of all—His Son Jesus—and we can count on Him to also *"freely give us ALL things"* we will ever need!

Let me pray for you...

> *Heavenly Father, thank You that You are a covenant-making, covenant-keeping God. Thank You that Your heart's desire is to release Your covenant blessings over this precious child of Yours. I ask today that You would prepare their heart to receive all You have in store for them. Prosper them, bless them with good health and strong relationships, and make them a blessing to others. I pray this in Jesus' name. Amen.*

Chapter 9

BLESSING KEY: *Two*

FOLLOW GOD'S FORMULA FOR A HARVEST OF BLESSINGS

In some ways, releasing God's blessings is simply a matter of following the *formula* or *recipe* He prescribes in His Word. You need the right ingredients, and it's important not to leave anything out!

When you were a young child, you probably learned simple, basic math equations. Well, I want to share with you a simple spiritual equation for releasing more of the treasures of Heaven into your life. It's so simple and easy to follow that you will see rapid changes in your life and your circumstances!

Let's look at the first half of this powerful spiritual equation—one so easy and simple that it can release the treasures of Heaven in your life. If you will faithfully follow this equation and put it into practice, God will bless your life in amazing ways.

Here's the first half of the equation:

FAITH + OBEDIENCE + EXPECTANCY

When added together, these three words provide the key to receiving God's breakthroughs and covenant blessings over your circumstances.

So what does this first half of the spiritual equation mean? Let me explain...

There have been many times when Barbara and I faced hard times and had to have faith that God would move powerfully on our behalf. In addition to putting our *faith* in the Lord, we chose to *obey* whatever He told us to do, and we then *expected* Him to bless us with His supernatural breakthroughs.

I remember one time in particular when our son Ben was an infant. He was burning up with a 104.5-degree fever. We called our pediatrician, who told us to bring Ben to the emergency room right away. He didn't say to bring him to his *office*, but to go immediately to the *emergency* room at the hospital. We knew it was serious!

Barbara and I were rushing out the door when I sensed the Holy Spirit's leading. I stopped and said to her, "Before we go, let's pray and anoint him with oil, and see what God will do."

So we sat down together on the couch with little Ben in our arms. As we anointed him with oil, we laid hands on him and prayed the prayer of faith together.

While we were praying, our baby boy literally went from burning up with fever to being completely cool, with no fever and a perfectly normal temperature. There was no longer any need for us to take him to the emergency room.

For two young parents with their first child, this was an amazing, miraculous breakthrough. We had used the simple spiritual equation of FAITH + OBEDIENCE + EXPECTANCY, and God blessed us with a complete turnaround in Ben's condition!

A Closer Look

Let's take a closer look at these three ingredients...

FAITH is the belief that God will intervene in our circumstances.

It involves confidence that if we love God, and called according to His purpose, He will cause all things to work together for our good (Romans 8:28). Just as with the other two ingredients, faith is an indispensable key to pleasing God and releasing His favor in our lives: "*Without faith it is **impossible** to please Him, for he who comes to God **must** believe that He is, and that He is a rewarder of those who diligently seek Him*" (Hebrews 11:6). Notice the words "*impossible*" and "*must*" here. Faith is the essential first step in receiving your miracle from God!

OBEDIENCE means putting our faith into action. This takes place when we:

Read God's Word and follow what it says and...

Listen to the voice of His Holy Spirit and obey what He tells us to do.

There is no substitute for obedience, for Jesus tells us, "*You are My friends if you do whatever I command you*" (John 15:14).

EXPECTANCY is a sense of hope-filled waiting, confident that our breakthrough is on the way. This only comes after we've prayed in faith, believing that God will intervene in our circumstances, and then are obedient to His Word and His Holy Spirit. We must wrap our faith and obedience with expectation, trusting Him to be faithful to His covenant promises.

In order for God to release His covenant blessings in our lives, He requires us to apply the formula of FAITH + OBEDIENCE + EXPECTANCY in every circumstance. We have *faith* in God's promises, we *obey* whatever He asks us to do, and then we *wait with expectation* for Him to stand behind His Word and provide the covenant blessings He has promised us.

Of course, I recognize how hard it can be to wait for your breakthrough from God. Yet in times of doubt or impatience, you need to remember these encouraging words from the prophet Jeremiah:

*The LORD's lovingkindnesses indeed never cease, for His compassions never fail. They are new every morning; great is Your faithfulness. "The LORD is my portion," says my soul, "Therefore I have hope in Him." The LORD is good to those who **wait** for Him, to the person who **seeks Him**. It is good that he **waits** silently for the salvation of the LORD* (Lamentations 3:22-26 NASB).

Sometimes people misunderstand what it means to wait upon the Lord. The word "wait" used in this passage is from the Hebrew word *qavah,* which means to wait with hope and expectancy. It's not meant to imply complacency or inaction, but rather an active trust in God to fulfill His promises.

This same word, *qavah,* is also used in Isaiah 40:31: *"Those who wait on the LORD shall renew their strength; they shall mount up with wings like eagles, they shall run and not be weary, they shall walk and not faint."* What a beautiful promise. Do you want to renew your strength? Are you looking for a way to soar above your problems? Do you need relief from weariness over the battles you've been facing? Then you need to wait on the Lord!

Numbers 23:19 (NASB) clearly tells us, *"God is not a man, that He should lie, nor a son of man, that He should repent; has He said, and will He not do it? Or has He spoken, and will He not make it good?"* So you can trust that God is who He says He is and that He will do what He says He will do. He promises to watch over His Word to perform it (Jeremiah 1:12).

The Bible is filled with examples of people in desperate situations who experienced supernatural breakthroughs when they applied FAITH + OBEDIENCE + EXPECTANCY:

A Gentile woman came to Jesus because her daughter was demon-possessed (Matthew 15:21-28). Testifying that the woman exhibited great faith, Jesus set her daughter free in a moment's time.

Jairus exercised his faith, obeyed, and expected Jesus to do a miracle on behalf of his daughter—raising her from the dead (Mark 5:22-43).

For 12 years, a woman had a bleeding problem, and she was unable to get any help from her doctors. But when she took action to approach Jesus with FAITH + OBEDIENCE + EXPECTANCY, she was instantly healed. Jesus told her, *"Your faith has made you whole"* (Mark 5:25-34).

Many other examples could be cited, but we need to move on to see what the spiritual equation will *produce* in our lives if we implement it...

The Second Half of the Equation

As we've already seen, God does amazing things in response to our FAITH + OBEDIENCE + EXPECTANCY. But what does all of this add up to? At times people in the Bible used this formula to receive a healing. At other times, they received a breakthrough in their finances or their family.

The good news is that this remarkable principle can be used to receive a supernatural breakthrough from God in WHATEVER area you need! How is this possible? Because God's harvest blessings can impact *every* area of your life.

You see, the full equation is this...

FAITH + OBEDIENCE + EXPECTANCY = GOD'S HARVEST OF BLESSINGS IN YOUR LIFE!

Let me give you an example of why this is so...

One of God's first recorded covenants in Scripture was given to Noah, who is described as *"a just man, perfect in his generations,"* a man who *"walked with God"* (Genesis 6:9). Because of Noah's faithfulness and obedience, God saved him and his family from the destruction of the flood that ended all other life on earth.

As the Lord did with other Biblical heroes, He framed His promises in terms of His faithfulness as a covenant God. He promised Noah, *"I will establish My covenant with you"* (Genesis 6:18).

As soon as the land was dry, the first thing Noah did was to honor God by building Him an altar and giving an offering...a sacrifice. God's heart was touched by Noah's actions, and He responded by making this powerful covenant with him: *"While the earth remains, seedtime and harvest, cold and heat, winter and summer, and day and night shall not cease"* (Genesis 8:22).

Isn't it amazing that one of the first recorded covenants in Scripture contains God's eternal principle of seedtime and harvest? When you chose to respond to God's love by inviting Jesus Christ to be your Lord, you entered into a covenant with Him, and ALL the blessings of Scripture became yours (Galatians 3:6-14).

Friend, the same covenant of seedtime and harvest that God made with Noah is still in effect for *you* today! But remember, a covenant is an agreement between two parties, just like the wedding vows Barbara and I made on our wedding day. In order for our covenant with one another to remain unbroken, *both* of us must remain faithful to our marriage vows.

Likewise, because of His great love with us, God has established His unending covenant of seedtime and harvest with us. **He will never fail to live up to His agreements and fulfill what He has promised to do!**

But what about *our* side of the covenant? What does God require of *us* in this covenant relationship?

The answer is found right in the first half of the equation: FAITH + OBEDIENCE + EXPECTANCY. Those are all "seeds" God asks us to sow into His Kingdom.

And what does He promise we will reap from these spiritual seeds? That's the second half of the equation...*His harvest of blessings*!

So let's look at God's Harvest Equation again:

**FAITH + OBEDIENCE + EXPECTANCY =
GOD'S HARVEST OF BLESSINGS IN YOUR LIFE!**

If you will allow God's Holy Spirit to impart this truth deep in your heart, then your life...your circumstances...your struggles...can all begin to turn around today!

An Ongoing Relationship

I've traveled all over the world and prayed for thousands of Believers. What I've observed is that many of God's children are experiencing life at a level far below the blessings He intends. All too often, they just live their lives on their own terms until they experience a crisis.

Perhaps you've met people like this. They lose their job...run out of money...get sick...or experience family conflicts before getting serious about their relationship with God. They wait until they get tangled in a cycle of defeat, depression, and despair...and *then* they cry out to God in desperation for Him to bless them.

In contrast, wouldn't life be so much better if you just chose to live in an ongoing relationship with God—experiencing an unending cycle of His blessings as a way of life? This is the kind of covenant living God wants you to experience. He has promised that His law of seedtime and harvest shall never cease, so the only thing that can go wrong is if we fail to fulfill *our* end of the covenant.

The simple, yet profound, truth is this: **God wants a relationship with us.** That's why He sent His Son to die on the Cross. Jesus was a seed God planted on the earth so that He could reap an eternal harvest of sons and daughters for His family.

Jesus told His disciples, *"Unless a grain of wheat falls into the ground and dies, it remains alone; but if it dies, it produces much grain"* (John 12:24).

The Lord was talking about *Himself*. He became the living, eternal proof that seedtime and harvest shall NEVER cease! And if Jesus is our Lord and Savior, then all of God's covenants and promises are ours in Him.

It's so simple really. God loves us. We love Him back, and we show our love for Him when we live for Him, put our faith in Him, obey Him, and expect Him to do what He has promised to do. God then responds by filling us with joy and pouring out His blessings over our lives.

And the cycle doesn't end there. God blesses us, not just for our own sake, but so we can be a blessing to others. As we give back to Him and sow into the lives of others, He gives us even *more*—until our life overflows with abundance. This is the unending cycle of covenant blessings God invites us to experience on a continual basis.

Obedient in the Little Things

Barbara and I regularly encourage our Inspiration Ministries partners to walk in a loving, obedient covenant relationship with the Lord, spending time with Him in prayer, worshiping Him, and reading the Scriptures each day. We also teach the importance of faithfully sowing seeds as they follow the leading of the Holy Spirit and wait expectantly to reap supernatural blessings.

But sadly, we often receive letters from those who have neglected their relationship with the Lord. Some are even openly living in sin while still asking God to reward their wrong choices with His blessings. Despite their disobedience, they seem puzzled by why they don't reap harvest blessings in their lives. They don't realize that if they want to experience God's blessings, they must consistently live in a loving, faith-filled, obedient relationship with Him.

Of course, most of us *do* try to be obedient to God in the "big" things of life. We don't murder anyone, don't have an affair with our neighbor's spouse, and don't rob any banks. But all too often, we're disobedient in "small" ways: unkind to loved ones or strangers, watching lust-filled TV programs or movies, gossiping about our friends, or cutting corners on our taxes.

However, God wants us to obey Him in both the big *AND* the small things. When we do, we will see Him move on our behalf as His Word so beautifully promises:

> *If you diligently obey the Lord your God, being careful to do all His commandments which I command you today, that the LORD will set you high above all the nations of the earth. **And all these blessings will come upon you and overtake you*** (Deuteronomy 28:1-2).

My friend, as you faithfully obey whatever God is calling you to do, you can trust Him to help and strengthen you. He is your loving Heavenly Father, and you are His child. Know that every act of obedience lessens the distance between you and the harvest you're waiting for God to supply!

The Lord's principle of seedtime and harvest is an eternal principle, and one you can confidently stand upon. As you faithfully and obediently walk in a covenant relationship with Him, you can have great expectations for your future and the wonderful plans God has for you!

Let me pray for you...

> *Heavenly Father, thank You for Your goodness and faithfulness to Your children. Thank You for offering to change our lives through Your covenant of seedtime and harvest. Move in the hearts and minds of everyone reading this book. Fill them with faith and the courage to obey. Cause hope to rise up within them as they expectantly wait on You to meet their every need and release Your covenant blessings in their life. I pray this in Jesus' name. Amen.*

Chapter 10

Everything Begins with a Seed

Seeds are pretty amazing, aren't they? Inside each one, God has deposited a specific DNA to determine what that seed will become. Every seed a farmer plants in good soil and carefully tends is destined to yield a fruitful harvest—and the same is true of the seeds of faith you sow into God's Kingdom.

Shortly after God set creation in motion, He made this powerful statement about the importance of seeds: *"Let the earth bring forth grass, the herb that **yields seed**, and the fruit tree that **yields fruit** according to its kind, whose **seed** is in itself, on the earth."* You see, in order for God to give us FRUIT, He first gives us SEEDS. And within the fruit He gives us as our harvest, there is an additional supply of seeds, enabling us to receive an even greater harvest in the future.

It's not an exaggeration to conclude that just about *everything* begins with a seed...

- An entire apple orchard began with just one apple seed.
- Amazing inventions began with the seed of an idea.
- Disneyland began with the seed of Walt Disney's vision.
- $1,000 in savings began with a seed of one dollar.
- Jesus' life on earth began with the seed of the Holy Spirit.
- Even *your life* began as a tiny, microscopic seed!

When Noah and his family stepped off the ark, they were entering into a whole new beginning for humankind. In the same way, no matter what kinds of trials you may have endured in the past, I'm convinced this can be YOUR day for a new beginning in your health, finances, emotions, or family.

But remember *how* the Lord instructed Noah to enter into the covenant blessings of his new life: through the law of seedtime and harvest! No wonder this was God's mechanism to bless Noah and his family, for every blessing and breakthrough begins with a seed.

In the natural realm, it's easy to understand the principle of sowing seeds and reaping a harvest. A farmer plants seeds, making sure the soil is healthy and well fertilized. He ensures that the seeds receive plenty of sun and water, and he endeavors to guard them from weeds and pestilence. As he diligently tends to his seeds, he knows they will produce a healthy and life-sustaining harvest.

Well, these same principles regarding seedtime and harvest are also true in the spiritual realm. First, you must take steps of faith to sow seeds into the good ground of God's Kingdom. And when you are diligent to fertilize the seeds with your faith, obedience, and expectancy, you can be confident you'll reap a bountiful harvest from God.

However, I realize that when times are hard, it's easy to get discouraged and become focused on what you *don't* have rather than what you *do* have. Perhaps you find yourself thinking, "I would love to give, but I barely have enough for my own needs." Or maybe you see a friend who needs assistance, but you say to yourself, "I'm just too tired to help."

This mindset is a common problem, preventing many Believers from receiving the breakthroughs they seek. Most people who are living in the lands of Not Enough or Barely Enough are taking inventory of their NEEDS...what they *don't* have...or what they *wished* they had. But if you truly want to live in God's Promised Land of More Than Enough, then it's time to take inventory of your SEEDS...what you *do* have!

Seeds of Many Kinds

What is a seed? I find that many people are confused about this. Often preachers talk about "financial seeds," but that is only one of many different kinds of seeds we can sow.

A seed is anything you've received *from* God that you can give back *to* God for Him to multiply. This means that even if you find yourself struggling today, you have more resources than you think. In fact, if you take a closer look, you're a *walking warehouse* of seeds!

Here is just a partial list of the kinds of seeds
you can sow into God's Kingdom:

❧ Love	❧ Patience	❧ Money
❧ Thoughts	❧ Talents	❧ Forgiveness
❧ Time	❧ Kindness	❧ Prayer
❧ Joy	❧ Gratitude	❧ Hope
❧ Faith	❧ Humor	❧ Help

Take a moment to do an inventory of the seeds God has already given you. Give Him thanks that you are already much richer than you thought!

Now that you've identified the seeds you've been given by the Lord, it's time to get excited about the potential harvest you can reap. Instead of concentrating on your present NEEDS, I challenge you to focus instead on your future harvest as you sow your SEEDS into the good ground of God's Kingdom.

Perhaps you've never stopped to consider how powerful your seed can be. However, when sown with faith, obedience, and expectancy, your seed can be energized by God to provide...

- An exit from your present!
- A door to your future!
- A bridge leading you out of the lands of Not Enough or Barely Enough to a land of More Than Enough, as the Lord releases His uncommon harvests!

Maybe you're thinking at this point, "But David, how do you *know* that God can do all these things through the seeds He's given me? After all, you don't even know the kinds of problems I'm dealing with."

But while it's true that I don't know the type of difficult situation you're facing today, I do know this: ***Everything begins with a seed.*** That means the principle of seedtime and harvest can give you a turnaround in ANY area of your life. Whether you need a financial breakthrough, a healing in your body, or the restoration of a broken relationship in your family, your seed can be exactly the KEY you've been looking for.

Too often, I see people who *withhold* their seed because of the size of their need. They think their problem is far too great for such a simple solution. However, this perspective is totally backwards. You should sow your seed *because* of your great need.

But this means you must stop focusing on what you DON'T have and concentrate instead on what you DO have. God has *already* given you powerful seeds to sow into His Kingdom. And when you take this step of faith and obedience, you can expectantly await a new beginning of God's covenant blessings in your life.

Uncommon Harvests

Perhaps you've heard the wise maxim, "If you *want* something you've never had, you must *do* something you've never done." I guess this is the flip side to the definition of insanity as "doing the same thing over and over, but expecting different results."

When I meet people facing dire needs, I'm astounded that they often are still doing the very things that have gotten them into the trouble they're in. Don't they see that it's time to do something *new* and *different*, taking an *uncommon step of faith* in expectation of an uncommon result?

When something is uncommon, it's unusual and different. Sometimes it even appears risky, because *faith* is involved. An uncommon seed is one that is out of the ordinary and unique. For example, it could be a financial seed that is above and beyond what you would typically give.

Actually, there are a number of different factors that can make a seed *uncommon*:

- A seed's *size* can make it UNCOMMON.
- A seed that requires great *sacrifice* is UNCOMMON.
- A seed sown in faith-filled *obedience* is UNCOMMON.
- A seed sown during a time of *crisis* or *hardship* is UNCOMMON.

While God can bless any seed you sow into His Kingdom, when a seed is uncommon it becomes magnified in His eyes. That's why an *uncommon seed* can be expected to produce an *uncommon harvest* of blessings.

So what makes a harvest blessing from God uncommon?

- The *size* of a harvest can make it UNCOMMON.
- A harvest that is clearly the result of an uncommon seed is UNCOMMON.
- A harvest that comes from an unexpected source is UNCOMMON.
- A harvest that you clearly couldn't produce on your own is UNCOMMON.

Why does God want you to sow uncommon seeds and reap His uncommon harvests? The answer is simple: *because He loves you*! Your Heavenly Father wants you to continuously live in His cycle of seedtime and harvest so He can abundantly bless you and enable you to become a greater blessing to others.

Remember, God is a covenant God, and He has declared that *"seedtime and harvest...shall not cease"* (Genesis 8:22). He stands behind His

Word, so the question is this: Will you trust Him, obey Him, and wait expectantly for His miracle harvests? Will you give Him uncommon seeds that He can multiply and transform into uncommon harvests?

An Uncommon Number: 58

Through the years, people have come up with different numbers for how many blessings are contained in Scripture, but I like to use the number 58. Perhaps you will find more or less, but that's how many I count.

One thing for sure is that *58 blessings* are a *lot*! And some of the specific covenant blessings are found in Isaiah *58*, verses 6-12. God promises such things as...

- Health (v. 8)
- Guidance / Wisdom (v. 11)
- Provision / Financial Favor (v. 11)
- Restored Relationships (v. 12)

God promises that these blessings are *yours....IF* you will be obedient to do what He asks of you in this passage: setting prisoners free, feeding the hungry, taking care of the poor, and reaching out with His compassion to those who are afflicted.

Isaiah 58 is a beautiful illustration of an important Biblical principle: When you get involved with God's dream, He gets involved with your dream. By generously partnering with Him to touch lives for Christ, you position yourself for an outpouring of His blessings.

Barbara and I have seen this principle at work over and over again in the lives of our Inspiration Partners. For example, as people sow seeds to reach lost people through our ministry outreaches, God gets involved in saving the *partners'* lost loved ones too. So remember: *What you have done to bless others, the Lord will do for you!*

Waiting for Your Harvest

One of the common misconceptions about the principle of seedtime and harvest is that you always will receive an *immediate* harvest for the seeds you sow. Although we've received thousands of testimonies from people who experienced this kind of immediate breakthrough, often seed-sowing Believers must patiently and expectantly *wait* for their harvest blessings to arrive.

Doesn't this make sense, after all? Just as a farmer must wait weeks or even months before he receives a harvest from the seeds he has planted, this is likewise true in God's Kingdom.

The Bible is perfectly clear about our need to patiently and expectantly WAIT for our miracle harvest to come: *"Let us not grow weary while doing good, for in due season we shall reap if we do not lose heart"* (Galatians 6:9). Notice the different aspects of this verse. On the one hand, we're promised that *"we SHALL reap."* That's good news! But on the other hand, we're told that our harvest will come *"in due season,"* and we must not *"lose heart"* while we're waiting.

Where are YOU right now in this process, my friend? If you've not planted any seeds, you can't expect a harvest. But if you HAVE sown seeds into God's Kingdom by faith, it's crucial that you continue to patiently believe Him for your harvest blessings.

Before closing this chapter, I want to leave you with a checklist of *7 vital steps* to review in order to be sure your harvest breakthrough is on the way:

1. Walk in a loving, obedient, faith-filled relationship with God.
2. Obey God's Word and the voice of His Holy Spirit.
3. Give each seed you sow a specific assignment for what you're asking God to do on your behalf.
4. Wrap your seeds with faith and expectancy.
5. Sow your uncommon seeds into good ground, continually and persistently.
6. Patiently wait to reap your harvest.
7. Thank God in advance, then honor Him with your testimony when you receive His uncommon harvests.

You can be confident God's promises are true. He wants to bless your finances, health, emotions, and relationships—and often He will do this through the powerful principle of seedtime and harvest:

> *He turns a wilderness into pools of water, and dry land into watersprings. There He makes the hungry dwell, that they may establish a city for a dwelling place, and sow fields and plant vineyards that they may yield a fruitful harvest. He also blesses them, and they multiply greatly* (Psalm 107:35-38).

Are you facing a barren wilderness in some area of your life today? He wants to quench your thirst and replace your emptiness with life-giving pools of water. But this is unlikely to happen until you *"sow fields and plant vineyards that they may yield a fruitful harvest."*

Let me pray for you...

> *Heavenly Father, we believe that Your Word is true and that You will never fail to honor Your covenant promises to us. I thank You for the many seeds You have placed in the hands of this child of Yours. Thank You that Your Word is filled with descriptions of the uncommon blessings they can receive as they continue to walk in a loving, faith-filled, obedient covenant relationship with You. Cause faith to rise in their heart as they listen to Your voice and respond to the leading of Your Holy Spirit regarding the seeds they can sow and the wonderful harvests they can reap. I pray this in Jesus' name. Amen.*

SMALL SEEDS CAN REAP GREAT HARVESTS

When a farmer plants a tiny corn seed, he typically ends up with millions of corn kernels. In the same way, when you sow seeds into God's Kingdom, He can multiply your seed into a harvest far greater than the original seed you sowed.

We see this principle throughout the pages of Scripture...

A shepherd brought his sling. A little boy brought his lunch. A widow brought her mite. Each of these heroes in the Bible offered to God what they had, and not only was it enough, but He made it *more* than enough! Because of their faith and obedience, the Lord honored their small seeds and created great harvests and huge blessings.

What seeds are you holding in your hand today? Do they seem small and insignificant? Just as God did with a shepherd, a little boy, and a needy widow, when you release the seed in *your* hand, He will release the harvest in *His* hand.

Don't miss this. A slingshot killed a giant. A lunch fed a multitude.

And a small offering has reached across the centuries to impact millions of Believers with the widow's example of generosity. So, if what you're holding in your hand seems insignificant...if it's too small to be your harvest...make it your *seed* instead! When you take a step of faith to plant what God has given you, He can multiply it beyond your wildest dreams.

Even Small Seeds Matter

When we're afraid we don't have enough, our tendency is to hoard what we *do* have. We fear that if we let go of the little we have, we'll end up with nothing. But in God's economy, the very opposite is true: He will take the little we give Him, bless it, multiply it, and give it back to us as an abundant harvest.

Zechariah 4:10 encourages us not to despise the day of *"small things."* Even if what we're giving to God seems incredibly small in our eyes, we must be willing to faithfully sow these humble gifts of our time, talent, or treasure back into His Kingdom. As with the widow's mite, the Lord knows how much or how little we have. What draws His attention is our willingness to trust and obey Him.

No matter how big or small your seed may be, keep in mind this central truth: **Seed faith is sowing something God has *given* in order to receive something He's *promised*.** That's why even a small seed, sown in faith and expectancy, can produce a HUGE harvest.

In his famous theory of relativity, Albert Einstein pointed out a similar principle in the field of physics. Until then, few people had any awareness of the enormous power locked away in ordinary atoms. But today nuclear power plants around the world are using the power of microscopically small atoms to light entire cities!

In the same way, God wants to show you the amazing power that can be generated by the seeds you are currently holding in your hands. When energized by God's favor and your faith, even the tiniest of seeds is packed with enough power to totally transform your circumstances!

However, just as most people were unaware of the hidden power stored in atoms, many people today have no idea of the miracle-working power locked away in their seeds. And the only way to truly find out is to take a step of faith and release the seed from their hands to God's hands.

So what seeds has God given YOU? You have far *more* seeds than you've ever realized before.

I encourage you, with God's help, to make a "Seed List" of the time, talent, and treasure He's given you. Don't worry about the *size* of the seeds, just write them down. And don't leave anything out!

Next, I want you to pray over this list. Ask the Lord to give you the desire, the opportunity, and the courage to faithfully sow the seeds He's given you, expecting an uncommon harvest in return. Remember: God wants to take even your smallest seeds and multiply them into a great harvest of blessings, for His Kingdom and in your personal life as well.

Does It Cost You Anything?

Although I've been emphasizing that the small size of a seed doesn't diminish its impact, it's crucial to recognize another side of the coin: While the SIZE of our gift doesn't matter to God, He *does* look for our SACRIFICE. You see, in order for our gift to truly be an uncommon seed, it must *cost us something*.

In 2 Samuel 24, King David had angered the Lord by counting the number of fighting soldiers he had available to him. While this might not seem like a big deal to us, God was angry because David's action had revealed pride and self-reliance rather than humble dependence on the Lord's provision and protection.

Convicted of his sin, David repented before the Lord, but his situation didn't turn around immediately. He still suffered the consequences of his choices, and God sent a plague that wiped out 70,000 of the 1,300,000 men David had been relying upon.

What could David do to end the plague? The prophet Gad instructed him to build an altar to the Lord on the threshing floor of a Jebusite named Araunah. When Araunah saw the king approaching, he bowed before him and said, *"Why has my lord the king come to his servant?"* (v. 21).

David replied, *"To buy the threshing floor from you, to build an altar to the LORD, that the plague may be withdrawn from the people."*

Araunah responded, *"Let my lord the king take and offer up whatever seems good to him. Look, here are oxen for burnt sacrifice, and threshing implements and the yokes of the oxen for wood. All these, O king, Araunah has given to the king. May the LORD your God accept you"* (v. 22-23).

But rather than accepting Araunah's offer to give him everything he needed to build the altar and make the sacrifice, David wisely said, *"No, but I will surely buy it from you for a **price**; nor will I offer burnt offerings to the LORD my God with that which **costs me nothing**"* (v. 24).

Scripture goes on to say, *"David bought the threshing floor and the oxen for fifty shekels of silver. And David built there an altar to the LORD, and offered burnt offerings and peace offerings. So the LORD heeded the prayers for the land, and the plague was withdrawn from Israel"* (v. 25).

Don't miss the powerful message in this story. David was the king, and he certainly could have demanded from Araunah anything he wanted. He could have built the altar and made the sacrifice to God for *free*. However, he knew his sacrifice had to **cost him something**. And because of his obedient, prayerful sacrifice, God stopped the plague.

In the same way, *our* sacrifices to God must cost *us* something. His focus is not on the size of our seeds, but whether they are truly sacrificial in nature. He sees our *heart* when we sow a seed. That's why even small and seemingly insignificant gifts are important to Him—IF they're important to *us*.

Big Doors, Small Hinges

Perhaps you don't have a very impressive seed to offer the Lord at the moment. But my friend, never underestimate God's power to change your life in an instant with something that seems too small to matter. Even in the physical realm, some of the most powerful forces are often controlled by tiny objects we may never see.

The Bible tells us that...

- A tiny rudder can turn a huge ship (James 3:4).
- The tongue is small, yet it's like a flame that can set an entire forest on fire (James 3:5).
- Mustard-seed faith can move a mountain (Matthew 17:20).
- The seemingly insignificant little town of Bethlehem became the birthplace of the Savior of the world (Matthew 2:4-6).

And I'm sure you could think of many examples of this principle in your own life. Your car is set in motion by a small key in the ignition switch. Light suddenly floods a dark home when you flip the light switch. Your shower is turned on by the mere twist of a faucet.

When people tell me about the major turning points of their lives, I'm often amazed to hear how a seemingly insignificant event impacted their entire life. This was certainly true for me. Over 40 years ago, I was in a discount department store in Tulsa, Oklahoma, buying some things to decorate my dorm room at Oral Roberts University when I struck up a conversation with the attractive checkout girl. Not a big deal, right? We just had a little chat to pass the time while she rang up my order.

How was I to know that this lovely young woman was going to be my wife and the mother of our children? That supposedly "chance" meeting and our small conversation changed our lives forever!

In the same way, a small seed may look insignificant in your eyes. Yet when God is involved, a little is all that is needed. He can cause big doors to swing on small hinges!

God knows that our NEED often seems a lot bigger than our SEED. This is why He reminds us that even the smallest of seeds—the mustard seed—grows into a *tree* (Luke 13:18-19). Just imagine...if God can take a tiny mustard seed and produce a tree, what kind of amazing harvest will

He produce from *your* small seed sown in faith?

So remember: You can trust Him to do BIG things even with a SMALL seed that is sown in faith, obedience, and expectancy.

Let me pray for you...

> *Heavenly Father, thank You that You love to bless Your children with uncommon harvests. Please take and multiply the seeds we bring You today, transforming them into great harvests that further Your Kingdom and meet our every need. I pray this in Jesus' name. Amen.*

Chapter 12

BLESSING KEY: *Five*

RELEASE THE SEED IN YOUR HAND

I once heard a story about two farmers facing hard times...

These two farmers—neighbors—looked out over their dry, dusty fields without much reason to hope. There'd been a drought the year before, and the money in the bank was nearly as dried up as the land in front of them.

But the coming year promised to be the worst yet. As another season of drought was predicted in the forecasts, both farmers turned their faces toward Heaven and asked God to send the rain.

Weeks passed. Still there was no rain. If asked, both of these men would have said they had faith in God to answer their prayers.

Yet only one of the farmers *did* something. He climbed on his tractor... plowed his fields...and planted seeds.

In time, God answered the farmers' prayers and sent the rain. But only *one* farmer reaped a harvest. Why? Because regardless of what he saw in the natural, he believed God would bless the seeds he had planted in faith. He released the seeds from *his* hand, and *God* released the harvest in His hand.

In the same way, it can be a real challenge to faithfully sow your financial seeds into God's Kingdom when you're faced with difficult economic times. If you're afraid of not having enough, you can be tempted to hold on to whatever you have. And then when the devil comes stalking you like a roaring lion seeking to devour your health, finances, or relationships (1 Peter 5:8), you cry out to God in desperation.

In contrast to this bleak scenario, God has a better plan. In order to confidently overcome the devil's attacks, you can maintain an uninterrupted cycle of "letting go" of your seeds by sowing bountifully into God's Kingdom. While the WORLD'S economic system tells you to *hoard*, GOD'S economy tells you to *give* (Luke 6:38).

Instead of hoarding your seeds, the Lord asks you to release back to Him what He has placed in your hands. Only then will you reap His full blessings in your life and be covered by His supernatural favor, provision, and protection.

God wants you to walk in a loving, obedient, faith-filled relationship with Him—and then He wants to bless your finances, health, and relationships. But never forget: *The Lord only can multiply what you sow, not what you hoard!*

So what kind of farmer are *you*? I encourage you to give each seed you sow a specific assignment for what you're asking the Lord to do on your behalf. Wrap your seeds with faith and expectancy, then wait patiently for your harvest. You will *surely* reap, so don't lose heart (Galatians 6:9).

Your Unused Jar of Seeds

Although it may sound obvious, I often find myself having to remind people that their seeds will never multiply or reproduce unless they first are SOWN.

Think about it this way...

Let's say you put a handful of seeds in a jar, place the jar in a cupboard, and leave it there for three months. When you come back, what will you find? A jar of seeds! Unless you had some soil and moisture in that jar, your seeds will be exactly the same as the day you put them there.

Just as you wouldn't discover any kind of harvest growing in your jar in the above scenario, the same is true of your spiritual seeds—such things as your time, talent, and treasure. In order for those seeds to sprout and become a harvest, you must plant them in healthy soil and water them with faith and expectancy. Only *then* can you expect to reap a supernatural harvest from God.

Don't allow the devil to steal your harvest by tempting you to hold on to your seeds. Unlike Satan, God is *NOT* a liar (Numbers 23:19). He speaks truth, and His Word teaches that if you want to receive more of His blessings in your life, you must GIVE. And if you want to reap miraculous harvests, you must SOW.

King Solomon, the wisest and richest man of his generation, said it this way:

> *One person gives freely, yet gains even more;*
> *another withholds unduly, but comes to poverty.*

> *A generous person will prosper;*
> *whoever refreshes others will be refreshed*
> (Proverbs 11:24-25 NIV).

You see, if you hold on to your seeds, you are choosing the road to poverty. But God promises that if you generously *sow* your seeds, you will gain even more than you started with. You will reap His abundant blessings and enter into His land of More Than Enough.

I also encourage you to be sure to *recognize* God's harvest of blessings when they come. For example, if your seed was sown in the form of money, that doesn't mean your harvest will come to you in that same form. Yes, often your supernatural harvest will come in the form of a financial breakthrough, but at other times your harvest will come in the form of a blessing that money can't buy—something like a restored relationship with a loved one.

When Your Harvest Is Delayed

Sometimes people tell me, "Well, I've tried that sowing and reaping stuff, David, and it just doesn't work for me. I've sown, but I haven't reaped. I've given, but received nothing in return."

Perhaps the problem is this, my friend: Sometimes you have to *wait* for your harvest. That's why Hebrews 6:12 instructs us to *"imitate those who through faith and patience inherit the promises."* Your *faith* will do little good if you lose heart and fail to exercise *patience* as well.

Galatians 6:9-10 reminds us not to lose heart in doing good, for we will reap in due time—at the right time—if we don't become weary and give up.

I can tell you from personal experience, *my* timing has almost never been *God's* timing. I've learned that we must be patient and keep doing the things we know to do...standing in faith, praying, being obedient to what God is telling us and having a spirit of expectation regardless of what we see happening with our natural eyes.

You also must recognize that you'll often face a *spiritual battle* for your harvest. It's in the context of this battle against the forces of darkness that Paul encourages us: *"Put on the full armor of God, so that when the day of evil comes, you may be able to **stand your ground**, and after you have **done everything**, to stand"* (Ephesians 6:13 NIV).

Notice that Paul says you will be able to stand your ground against the enemy's attacks when you've *"done everything."* In other words, to be victorious in spiritual warfare and experience the full measure of God's blessings, it's crucial to obey His instructions. For example, if you haven't sown any seeds, you're probably waiting for your harvest in vain!

An Unending, Bountiful Harvest

God Himself is the ultimate Giver. As John 3:16 so beautifully describes, He loved you and me so much that He GAVE His only Son. And He did this because He knew that was the only way to reap a harvest of *other* sons and daughters for His family (Hebrews 2:10).

God initiated an unending cycle of giving and receiving by giving us His Son to be our Savior and then giving us His Holy Spirit to be our Comforter and Guide. Everything we have is because of His compassion and generosity.

If God is such a sacrificial Giver and Sower, shouldn't we respond to His love by following His example? Everything we have, we only have because He has given it to us. And He wants us to express our gratitude and trust by giving back to Him a portion of what we've received from Him (Malachi 3:8-10).

When we're faithful in giving Him what is rightfully His, God then gives us more, and we give more back to Him. As this cycle of covenant faithfulness continues, the Lord blesses us with *more and more*—until we're living in His amazing land of More Than Enough.

What a great God! Whenever we let go of what we're holding on to, our Heavenly Father replaces it with something better. It's impossible to out-give Him, because His very *nature* is to give! How could it be otherwise, when the Bible says of Him, *"God IS love"* (1 John 4:8)?

So remember: God has established His eternal principle of sowing and reaping, and He never interrupts this cycle. But sadly, *we* do at times. And when that happens, our harvests get interrupted because of delays in our sowing.

Sometimes I run into people who tell me they just don't have *anything* to sow into the Kingdom. Well, that's simply not true. Each of us has a measure of *something*. We have *some* time. We have *some* talent. We have *some* treasure. We have *some* seed to sow.

We're promised in 2 Corinthians 9:10 that God will give *"seed to the sower."* Notice that this isn't a blanket promise to give seed to just *anyone*. Rather, God is saying He will be faithful to supply us with seeds IF we have a heart of obedience to sow into His Kingdom.

My friend, don't allow the enemy to sow seeds of doubt in your mind.

When you commit to sowing uncommon seeds into God's Kingdom, you are being an obedient *doer* of the word and not a *hearer* only (James 1:22). After you've released the seeds in your hand to the Lord, your heart will be full of excitement while you expectantly wait to reap His supernatural harvests in your life.

Don't procrastinate or delay! The sooner you get your seed into the good ground of God's Kingdom, the sooner you'll receive your harvest blessings.

Let me pray for you...

Heavenly Father, we want to be like the farmer who planted seeds, even in the midst of drought. Give us that kind of faith in Your power to bless and multiply our seeds. Father, we trust in You and thank You for Your great love. Help this child of Yours to sow bountifully into Your Kingdom, so that they will reap bountifully of Your harvest blessings. Give them the courage and the hope to release the seeds You've placed in their hands so that You can release the amazing harvests in Your hand. I pray this in Jesus' name. Amen.

Chapter 13

BLESSING KEY: *Six*

SOW INTO GOOD GROUND

If you've ever taken a car ride through the countryside, you've probably passed acre after acre of abundant, thriving farmland. It's a beautiful thing to see healthy green crops springing up out of rich, dark earth.

But bountiful harvests like that don't just happen, do they? Behind every ripe harvest field stands a wise farmer who has carefully cultivated and prepared that ground before ever planting a single seed.

He spent time removing the rocks, putting proper nutrients into the soil, and making sure there would be proper irrigation and drainage. Knowing that seed is *costly*, he was diligent to maximize the harvest he expected his land to yield. No wonder he did everything he could to ensure a good harvest *before* sowing his precious seed into the ground.

How does the farmer know whether or not he made a wise decision about his soil? By the harvest he reaps in the fall! If he has been a wise steward of his resources, at harvest time he will end up living in the land of More Than Enough. However, if he has foolishly sown into poor soil, he will find himself in the lands of Not Enough or Barely Enough.

Jesus perfectly illustrates the value of sowing seed into good ground in the parable He told about the sower who went out to sow (Matthew 13:3-23). Some of the seeds fell by the wayside, and birds came and ate them. Other seeds fell on stony ground and eventually withered away because they couldn't put down strong, healthy roots. And still other seeds fell on thorny ground and got choked out.

However, some of the seeds reaped a bountiful harvest—not because of the quality of the seeds, but because of the soil they were planted in. Jesus explained that some of the seeds fell on *"good ground and yielded a crop; some a hundredfold, some sixty, some thirty."* That's a great harvest!

After telling the story, Jesus gave His disciples this explanation: *"The seed that fell on good soil represents those who truly hear and understand God's word and produce a harvest of thirty, sixty, or even a hundred times as much as had been planted!"* (v. 23 NLT).

Look how remarkable this is, my friend. Jesus said that seed sown into good soil could reap *"even a hundred times as much as had been planted."* That's an amazing return on the investment, isn't it?

The Message paraphrase says the good ground *"produces a harvest beyond his wildest dreams."* Wouldn't YOU like to receive that kind of harvest from the seeds you sow into God's Kingdom?

Is All Soil *GOOD* Ground?

Keep in mind that not all soil yields the same level of harvest. And just because it may look good at first glance, closer examination may reveal that the spiritual ground is dry, infested, rocky, hard, or unproductive.

This principle explains why some people seem to sow so faithfully, yet receive only a meager harvest. The quantity and quality of their harvest was impacted by the poor quality of the soil where their seeds were planted.

So the undeniable conclusion is this:

YOUR SEED + POOR SOIL = A POOR HARVEST!

YOUR SEED + GOOD GROUND = A GREAT HARVEST!

Why would you want to waste your prayers and financial seeds by sowing them into soil that isn't going to yield a fruitful harvest? This would be a regrettable outcome, both in your personal life, and even more importantly, for God's eternal Kingdom. It's like an ill-advised stock investor who doesn't take time to research the funds where his money is being placed.

Seeds are too precious to waste! If you're like me, you want to sow your seeds into soil where you'll reap the greatest rewards personally, and where you impact the most lives for Christ. And Jesus promises that good ground can enable the seeds of your time, talent, and treasure to reap a 100-fold return.

So I encourage you to be a wise and faithful sower. It's important to sow your uncommon seeds into ground that will produce the greatest amount of fruit!

Earmarks of Good Ground

One of the stunning lessons in this parable is that not all good ground is the same. Some produce a 30-fold return, some 60, and some a 100-fold return. But how does this apply to you and me?

When a ministry is truly yielded to God, it becomes good ground for sowing. The more a ministry is aligned with God's will and anointed by His Spirit, the more fruit it will bear. And partners of such a ministry will reap a greater harvest as well.

Since you're promised a great harvest when you sow into good ground, you should ask yourself some important questions about any church or ministry where you are considering sowing your precious seeds:

- Is Jesus Christ exalted as Lord and Savior?
- Is the Word of God preached without compromise?
- Is honor given to the Holy Spirit and His gifts and fruit?
- Is there eternal impact in the form of lost people being saved and Believers being discipled?
- Is there evidence of genuine love for the Lord and others?

If your answer to even one of these questions is "No" when you're considering a particular church or ministry, then you probably don't want to waste your precious seeds by sowing them there. In all likelihood, that would be sowing into rocky, hard, or unproductive soil.

However, if you can answer a resounding "Yes!" to all of these questions, then you most likely have found good soil where you can faithfully sow your seeds. You can sow with faith and expectancy, trusting God to release the supernatural harvests He has destined for your life.

Just remember that *TIME* is a key ingredient between sowing and reaping. You can't plant a garden today and make a salad tomorrow! In the same way that seeds in the natural take time to produce a harvest, the uncommon seeds you sow into God's Kingdom usually take time to mature into His uncommon harvests in your life.

When you patiently wait, you will joyfully reap. You can stand by faith on this great promise from God: *"Those who sow in tears shall reap in joy. He who continually goes forth weeping, bearing seed for sowing, shall doubtless come again with rejoicing, bringing his sheaves with him"* (Psalm 126:5-6).

Notice the wonderful word *"doubtless"* in this passage. God promises that when you sow seeds into His Kingdom and water them with your love, faith, and obedience, you will *surely* reap His harvest of blessings with great joy!

Sow Where You Are Nourished

As you prayerfully consider where to sow your financial seeds, an important factor is to support ministries where you are being spiritually fed.

Malachi 3:10 tells us to bring our tithes into *"the storehouse."* Many Christians have been taught that the storehouse is limited to the local church. I believe this is an inaccurate application of what the storehouse represented in Scripture.

The Bible describes the storehouse as a place where things were kept for the service, offerings, and sacrifices of the Temple. When something was needed for the Temple, for the work of God, the priests would go into the storehouse to retrieve some of the resources that had been deposited there.

The message for us is clear: You have a spiritual account in Heaven, and every time you sow your financial seeds into the good ground of God's Kingdom, you are storing up treasures in that account. When you need something in your life, there should be spiritual "storehouses" where you've made deposits you can draw upon.

Think of it this way...

When you eat lunch at McDonald's, you don't go across the street to Wendy's to pay for your meal. Yet this is exactly what many Christians do when they sow their financial seeds into churches or ministries that aren't feeding them spiritually.

I'll never forget one man's response when I asked why he had planted a large seed into Inspiration Ministries. He told me, "David, it's because I eat at your table every day!" So the answer to the question of "Where should I give my tithes and offerings?" is this: Give where you are being spiritually fed!

If you're being fed by your local church and by one or more different ministries, then I believe you should divide your seeds—your tithes and your offerings—among them. I encourage you to sow your seeds into ministries that are not only fulfilling the Great Commission, but also nourishing your own spiritual life.

Why is this so important? For one thing, it's because your spiritual vitality is a key to living in the land of More Than Enough. Ministries that build up your faith to receive God's promises are a vital ingredient in this equation.

Let me pray for you...

Heavenly Father, thank You for Your Word that is so full of wisdom for us regarding sowing and reaping. Make us wise stewards of the seeds You have entrusted to us. Please give this child of Yours the ability to recognize the good ground that You have prepared to receive their precious seeds. As they sow into Your Kingdom, I ask that You would cause their seeds to reap a 100-fold return, both in their personal life and in bringing more Souls into Your Kingdom. May they be greatly blessed, so that they may BE a great blessing to others. I pray this in Jesus' name. Amen.

Chapter 14

BLESSING KEY: *Seven*

GIVE YOUR SEED A SPECIFIC ASSIGNMENT

In the natural world, God has authorized seeds to mature into a harvest by assigning each one a specific set of invisible genetic instructions called DNA to determine what it will be when it matures. Because of these preordained assignments...

- An acorn becomes an oak tree.
- An apple seed becomes an apple tree.
- A father's seed becomes a child.

There's nothing random or haphazard about this process. If you know the DNA of a seed, you can get an accurate picture of its destiny.

In the same way, you must give your seeds authority to multiply and grow into a harvest by giving them a *spiritual* DNA—a specific assignment—for the harvest you want to reap. There's a powerful story in 1 Kings 17 that illustrates this simple principle.

God had led the prophet Elijah into the wilderness to live by the Brook Cherith. There the Lord had provided him with rest, food, and water. But eventually the water in the stream dried up because of the severe drought in the land. So the Lord sent Elijah to Zarephath and told him a widow there would provide for him.

Elijah obeyed God, and by the time he got to Zarephath, he was thirsty and hungry. When he encountered the widow, she was gathering sticks to make a fire, and he asked her for a drink of water and something to eat.

Due to the drought and famine, however, the widow's situation was desperate. All of her resources—her husband, her money, even her hope for any kind of future—were gone. According to verse 12, she had just enough flour in her bowl and oil in her jar to make a morsel of bread for herself and her son. And then she assumed both of them were going to starve to death:

> As the LORD your God lives, I have no bread, only a handful
> of flour in the bowl and a little oil in the jar; and behold, I am
> gathering a few sticks that I may go in and prepare for me and my
> son, that we may eat it and die (v. 12).

Elijah's response to her terrible situation was pretty startling. Rather than feeling sorry for her or trying to find something for her to eat, he told her to make some bread for *him* first, and *then* make something for her and her son out of whatever was left. Elijah promised the woman if she would listen to what he told her to do, her bowl of flour and her jar of oil would not run out:

> Do not fear; go, do as you have said, but make me a little bread
> cake from it first and bring it out to me, and afterward you may
> make one for yourself and for your son. For thus says the LORD
> God of Israel, "The bowl of flour shall not be exhausted, nor shall
> the jar of oil be empty, until the day that the LORD sends rain on
> the face of the earth" (vs. 13-14).

The widow must have wondered if Elijah was crazy. However, since she was going to die anyway unless God did a miracle, her desperation overcame any skepticism. We read in verses 15 and 16:

> So she went and **did** according to the word of Elijah, and she and
> he and her household ate for many days. The bowl of flour was

not exhausted nor did the jar of oil become empty, according to the word of the LORD which He spoke through Elijah.

What a great example of someone who sowed a seed during a time of incredible lack! As a result, the widow miraculously received an incredible release of prosperity and blessing from the Lord. She and her son *"ate for many days"* on that handful of flour and small amount of oil! As this faithful woman obeyed the word from God's prophet, she and her household received a harvest of supernatural abundance.

Making the Right Choice

The prophet's audacious request to provide for him before meeting her needs and the needs of her son must have seemed greedy and selfish to this desperate mother. His instructions seemed not only difficult, but impossible. Not to mention foolish!

But God had a different perspective. He wasn't planning this woman's demise. Far from it. He had an uncommon harvest on His mind for her, and so He had sent His prophet to her with a life-changing instruction—one she could either obey or ignore.

At that critical moment, this desperate mother had a choice to make. She could believe what the man of God told her to do, or she could have one last meal with her son and then wait for them both to die.

We all face defining moments in life from time to time, and this was certainly one for this poor widow. No one could have blamed her if she said, "No!" She no doubt was tempted to tell Elijah, "Leave me alone!" And most of us would have firmly replied, "Go get your *own* bread!"

But the woman didn't say any of these things. She chose to believe Elijah, obey his instruction, and then wait with hope-filled expectation for what the man of God had promised to come true.

Because Elijah knew the widow's handful of flour and few drops of oil weren't enough to be a life-sustaining harvest, he had given authority to the flour and oil to become SEEDS—with a *specific assignment* to grow and multiply. Speaking with faith and expectancy, he declared that God would take them and turn them into a bountiful harvest of provision for this little family.

Because this woman made the right choice and sowed an uncommon seed in the face of her desperate need, she miraculously went from having not enough to having *more* than enough. Instead of facing an untimely death, she and her son could enjoy an abundant life.

Rather than surrendering to fear and unbelief, the widow chose to trust the Lord and release what was in her hand. The result? Miraculous provision as God released His harvest blessings into her desperate circumstances.

Had the woman chosen to hoard the little bit in her hands, the consequences would have been terrible. But because of her step of faith, this mother and son ate, and ate well, for many days. Throughout the remaining years of drought and famine, her flour was never used up, and her oil never ran dry.

Think of it: an *inexhaustible* supply of resources! She had tapped into God's covenant blessings, which enabled her to live in the land of More Than Enough.

Your Future Is in Your Hands!

My friend, I pray you will follow this widow's example today. May you reject fear and choose faith. May you choose to believe and obey the promises of God.

When you choose to trust God with your resources—meager as they may seem—you can experience this same kind of blessing. Whatever your need may be—whether financial provision, healing, peace of mind, or restoration of a relationship—your covenant God will demonstrate His endless love and faithfully meet your need.

Just as He showed the widow, God has an *unlimited* supply for *YOU.* In the midst of the difficult circumstances you're facing, you can obey His Word and trust that all of His promises are for you. Your future will be determined by whether you believe and obey the Lord's instructions. Your faith-filled obedience can be the difference between poverty and prosperity, stress and rest, and even between death and life.

As long as you hold on to your seed, you will never experience a harvest greater than what you're holding. But as you release the seed in your hand, God will release the harvest in *His* hand. When you put the Lord first—looking to Him as your Source and giving out of your need, as the widow did—you can expect Him to move supernaturally in your situation (Matthew 6:33).

So ask yourself this important question: Is there a specific harvest you need to reap? Then do what Elijah did. When you sow your seeds, be sure to give them authority and a specific assignment for the breakthrough you need. The same God who multiplied the flour and oil for the widow will supernaturally multiply what *you* sow and supply whatever *you* need!

By giving your seed a specific assignment, you're attaching a spiritual DNA, authorizing it to accomplish a certain purpose. Don't be afraid to ask God for something that seems BIG and miraculous. He *specializes* in answering prayers like that!

Your seed's assignment can be for a physical healing, whether for you or for a loved one. You also can sow your seed for the restoration of a relationship or for the wisdom you need for an important decision. Or perhaps you need a financial breakthrough or a new job. Whatever area of your life needs God's supernatural intervention, make that the specific assignment of your seed.

Also, make sure to consistently water your seed with faith, obedience, and expectation for God to do what He says in His Word He'll do. Then watch Him step into your circumstances as He releases His uncommon harvests in your life!

Let me pray for you...

Heavenly Father, thank You for using the natural world to teach us powerful spiritual lessons. We believe in Your goodness, love, and faithfulness as we trust You and sow our seeds into Your Kingdom. I pray the Prayer of Agreement from Matthew 18:19, believing that as this child of Yours gives their seed a specific assignment, they will reap exactly the breakthrough they need. We thank You in advance for the miracles You are about to unleash. I pray this in Jesus' name. Amen.

Chapter 15

BLESSING KEY: *Eight*

MAKE THINGS HAPPEN FOR OTHERS

Do you remember the Golden Rule you were taught as a child? Perhaps you were mean to another kid, and your father or mother sternly reprimanded you, "Do unto others as you would have them do unto you!"

Your parents were teaching you that you needed to treat others the same way you wanted to be treated. You were to share your toys with others, because you wanted them to share their toys with you. And you needed to refrain from kicking or punching the other kids, because you surely didn't want them to kick or punch you.

Aren't you glad someone took time to teach you this important principle? It is taken directly from Jesus' words in Matthew 7:12, and it applies whether you're a kid on the playground or an adult on the job.

But God's Word *also* includes a similar golden rule—one that specifically applies to sowing seeds and reaping His uncommon harvests. Ephesians 6:7-8 says:

*With goodwill doing service as to the Lord, and not to men, knowing that **whatever good anyone does, he will receive the same from the Lord*** (Ephesians 6:7-8).

Do you see how powerful this is? Whatever good you make happen for *others*, God makes happen for *you*!

The Bible is full of stories demonstrating this principle, but here are just a few examples:

- God blessed Abraham and Sarah with a child of their own *after* they prayed for God to remove barrenness from the king's household (Genesis 20).
- God honored King David's life *after* he honored the life of King Saul (1 Samuel 26).
- God gave Nehemiah authority and resources for rebuilding Jerusalem's walls *after* he faithfully served in the house of a pagan king (Nehemiah 2).

Another Kind of Seed-Sowing

In previous chapters, I've mentioned the importance of sowing seeds into Gospel-preaching ministries and churches, but there is *another* kind of seed-sowing described in God's Word: We're to serve the Lord by doing good things for *others*; and when we do, He will do good things for *us*.

This means that when we sow seeds of our time, talent, and treasure into the lives of other people, we will reap supernatural harvests from God. As we bless others—our family, friends, pastor, church, coworkers, boss, and, yes, even our enemies—the Lord blesses us abundantly in return.

Amazingly, God looks at this kind of sowing as being equivalent to sowing seeds directly into His Kingdom. That's why the Bible says, *"If you help the poor, you are lending to the LORD—and he will repay you!"* (Proverbs 19:17 NLT). God treats your assistance to the poor as a loan to

HIM, and He promises to repay it.

We see this again when Jesus describes a scene at the final judgment, when He will commend His faithful followers: *"I was hungry and you gave Me food; I was thirsty and you gave Me drink; I was a stranger and you took Me in; I was naked and you clothed Me; I was sick and you visited Me; I was in prison and you came to Me"* (Matthew 25:35-36).

Those who hear these beautiful words of affirmation will be puzzled, Jesus says. They simply don't remember ever seeing the Lord in that kind of condition. When did they do any such things to minister to Him in His time of need?

Jesus then gives this stunning explanation: *"The King will answer and say to them, 'Assuredly, I say to you, inasmuch as you did it to one of the least of these My brethren, **you did it to Me**'"* (Matthew 25:40).

What a fantastic picture of how God shows us His favor as we sow into the lives of others.

Ruth's Surprising Harvest

This same truth is evident in the story of a simple country girl from the plains of Moab.

We learn in the book of Ruth that Naomi and her husband Elimelech, along with their two sons Mahlon and Chilion, lived in Bethlehem, a town in Judah. However, when a terrible famine struck the land, the family moved to the neighboring country of Moab, hoping for a better life.

Yet the hard times didn't end there. In fact, things grew worse...much worse. First, Elimelech died, and Naomi was left a widow. But at least she had her two sons.

However, after marrying two Moabite women—Ruth and Orpah—Naomi's two sons died as well. This left her without a husband or children, living a long distance away from any relatives.

Naomi wanted no more of the suffering she had encountered in Moab. When she heard the famine had ended in her own country, she decided to return home. Instructing her daughters-in-law to return to their own families, Naomi intended to travel back to Bethlehem alone. But while Orpah reluctantly went back to her own people, Ruth refused to leave her mother-in-law.

Even though her own husband had also died, Ruth rejected the easy road of finding a new husband in Moab. Instead, she chose to follow her mother-in-law Naomi to an unfamiliar place. Even though Naomi was bitter and going through a dark time in her life, Ruth refused to leave her, no matter how tough things got.

Throughout the story, Ruth repeatedly demonstrated her loving dedication and devotion to Naomi. She worked hard in the fields to bring home food and showed tremendous respect for her mother-in-law. Her unswerving faithfulness in standing by Naomi led the women of the Bethlehem community to comment that Ruth was *"better to (her) than seven sons"* (4:15).

Ruth endured much adversity in order to bless Naomi. And what was the outcome? In the midst of her suffering, ***God blessed Ruth.***

Naomi had a relative, Boaz, who was *"a man of standing"* (2:1). Not only did he help Ruth as she gathered grain in his fields, but he chose to "redeem" the family land from Naomi and marry Ruth. God eventually gave Ruth and Boaz a son, and through him the lineage of King David was established—the same lineage that led to Jesus Christ, the Savior of the world.

Not only did Ruth prosper in her own day, but she also continues to be honored for her faithfulness and remembered thousands of years beyond her lifetime. What an uncommon harvest. ***Because Ruth chose to bless Naomi, God chose to bless Ruth in return.***

Who Are YOU Blessing?

Friend, if you want the Lord to bless you with His supernatural harvests, I encourage you to be a blessing to others as you sow seeds of love, kindness, or finances into their lives. When YOU bless others, HE will bless you!

The message is clear: Do you want God to bless you? Then *be* a blessing to others! Be *other*-centered rather than *self*-centered. Get involved with someone else's dream, and God will get involved with *your* dream!

When considering what it means to BE a blessing, I encourage you to ask yourself whether you are a *problem creator* or a *problem solver*. Look at the difference:

A problem creator...

- Makes life harder for those around them
- Creates mountains out of molehills
- Criticizes, judges, and discourages others
- Demands that others bless *them*

A problem solver...

- Makes life easier for those around them
- Creates molehills out of mountains
- Affirms, accepts, and encourages others
- Seeks to *bless* others rather than *take* from them

In every circumstance, you can choose to make a situation better or worse. You can be an encourager or a discourager. You can offer compassionate assistance, or you can withhold your help.

Do you want God to bless you? Then continually look for ways to bless others!

But while you are doing this, keep in mind that your harvest will come from *God*, not necessarily from the person you've blessed. He will ask you to sow into another's field, and when it's His time for you to receive your harvest, you'll most likely reap from a different field. But all along the way, keep looking to HIM! He will give you exactly the harvest you *need*, not necessarily the same kind of seed you have sown.

Never forget: *ALL* harvests belong to God. As King David gratefully exclaimed, *"Yours, O LORD, is the greatness, the power and the glory, the victory and the majesty; for ALL that is in heaven and in earth is Yours"* (1 Chronicles 29:11).

God alone determines when—and where—you will reap.

Let me pray for you...

Heavenly Father, thank You that You have created us in Your image and made us to be like You. I ask You to help this child of Yours to grow more and more into Your likeness. Just as You love to bless us, may You increase their desire to glorify You by BEING a blessing to others. May the seeds of time, treasure, and talent they sow into the lives of others be multiplied and returned back to them, both in this present life and in eternity. I pray this in Jesus' name. Amen.

Chapter 16

BLESSING KEY: *Nine*

WAGE WAR WITH THE ENEMY

The devil hates God's principle of seedtime and harvest! Instead of wanting you to enjoy God's harvest blessings of power, peace, and provision, he comes to *"steal, kill, and destroy"* (John 10:10). He tries to devour your God-given seed, rob you of your blessings, and leave you in bondage to fear and financial lack.

If you listen to the enemy's lies, you'll hear a message like this: "You might as well get *used* to living in the lands of Not Enough or Barely Enough, because that's your destiny in life! Don't bother dreaming of anything better than that."

But remember God's original intention for humankind, described in the first chapters of Genesis. Creation was so awesome that *"God saw everything that He had made, and indeed it was very good"* (Genesis 1:31).

In those early days, God walked with Adam and Eve in the beautiful garden He had made for them. He fulfilled every need and gave them dominion over everything He had made. It was a life without sickness, sadness, strife, poverty, or death.

But Satan was jealous of the favor God showed to the man and woman, and he set out to deceive and control them. Genesis 3:1 says, *"The serpent was more cunning than any beast of the field,"* and he immediately began raising questions about whether God could be trusted.

Rather than saying, *"Get behind me, Satan!"* (Matthew 16:23), Adam and Eve took the enemy's bait—hook, line, and sinker. Doubting God's faithfulness and His love for them, they ate from the forbidden tree and tried to hide from God. As a result, they suffered the natural consequences of their turning away from Him—losing their previous abundance and intimacy with the Lord.

From the very beginning of creation, we see the devil's vendetta against humankind. Time and time again, he has used lies and manipulation to rob the people of God of their intended blessings. Too often, we have failed to discern the enemy's schemes and have neglected to exercise our God-given authority over him.

Put simply, the devil is real, and he doesn't want you to be blessed. He is a liar and the father of all lies (John 8:44). His goal is to undermine our confidence in the truth of God's Word. When that happens, we fail to appropriate the covenant blessings that could be ours.

The Attack on Your Seeds

Satan knows that if he can devour your seeds or trick you into hoarding them, you will never receive the harvest blessings God wants you to have. He has utilized this same strategy repeatedly throughout time:

Moses was God's seed, the deliverer He would raise up to lead the Israelites to freedom in the Promised Land. So when Moses was born, Satan tried to devour God's seed by killing all the Jewish male babies (Exodus 1:15-17).

Jesus was God's seed, sent to die for our sins and lead all Believers to eternal freedom in our Promised Land in Heaven. So when Jesus was born, Satan tried to devour God's seed by once again murdering thousands of Jewish male babies (Matthew 2:16-18).

In Revelation 12, we see a similar scene when *"the dragon [Satan] stood before the woman who was ready to give birth, to devour her Child as soon as it was born"* (v. 4). Again, the devil's plot to devour this seed was foiled, and we're later given a powerful formula for our *own* victory over the enemy: *"They overcame him by the blood of the Lamb and by the word of their testimony, and they did not love their lives to the death"* (v. 11).

Do you see the recurrent pattern in these examples? Satan repeatedly tries to abort God's harvest by devouring the seeds He provides. And make no mistake about it, Satan is *still* trying to devour *your* God-given seeds and rob *you* of God's harvest blessings of power, peace, and provision.

However, the good news is that Satan is a defeated foe. You don't have to allow him to rob you of your seed and your intended harvest.

Yes, Satan *WAS* the ruler of this world. He *HAD* dominion over the earth. But through Jesus' sinless life, sacrificial death on the Cross, and resurrection from the dead, He stripped Satan of his authority and returned to us the authority lost when Adam and Eve sinned in the Garden.

Paul writes that Jesus *"disarmed the powers and authorities, he made a public spectacle of them, triumphing over them by the cross"* (Colossians 2:15 NIV). This means you don't have to let the devil push you around. In Christ, you are more than a conqueror (Romans 8:37), destined to live in the land of More Than Enough!

Get Ready to Fight

When God brought the Israelites into their Promised Land—the land of More Than Enough—they were startled to find that some *battles* still had to take place before they could live at peace there.

Never forget...

Seedtime and harvest is a battle, and the enemy will wage a fierce war against the blessings God wants to give you as a result of your obedience to Him!

But the good news is that when Jesus is your Lord and Savior and you're walking in an obedient covenant relationship with Him, you have the right to take *authority* over the enemy. You have the right to command Satan to leave, and you don't have to let him rule over you! You must never forget Jesus' promise, *"Behold, I have given you authority to tread on serpents and scorpions, and over ALL the power of the enemy"* (Luke 10:19). You must take the battle to devil—without fear!

Many Believers today don't realize their need to wage war with the enemy in order for their seed to become a bountiful harvest. Sadly, many are passive when it comes to spiritual warfare, and the devil is having a heyday in their health, finances, and relationships.

Friend, you can't remain on the defensive when it comes to spiritual warfare. Jesus warned that the Kingdom of Heaven suffers violence, and violent people take it by force (Matthew 11:12). That means you'll never find victory if you just sit back and wait for the enemy to attack. Instead of having a *defensive* strategy against the enemy, you must have an *offensive* battle plan to protect what is rightfully yours as God's child—taking back whatever the devil has stolen from you!

God has given you all the tools you need to win the battle for your harvest:

> *No weapon formed against you shall prosper, and every tongue which rises against you in judgment you shall condemn. This is the heritage of the servants of the Lord* (Isaiah 54:17).

What a powerful truth! Satan's weapons and accusations are demolished when Christ lives in you and you stand in His authority. You have *His* strength, *His* power, and *His* righteousness to use against the devil.

But you have a choice today. You can sit back and do nothing, letting the enemy devour your seed and destroy your harvest. Or you can take up your weapons of spiritual warfare and wage war against him in Jesus' mighty name.

I'm praying that you will learn to walk in Jesus' authority and enjoy all the benefits of a faith-filled, obedient covenant relationship with your Heavenly Father. You don't have to fear the devil's tactics, for the Bible promises you victory when you do what it says: *"Submit to God. Resist the devil and he will flee from you"* (James 4:7).

Don't give up! Though the battle for your breakthrough may be fierce at times, God will enable you to WIN.

Let me pray for you...

> *Heavenly Father, thank You that You have not left us alone or defenseless against the devil's attacks. According to Psalm 18, You arm us with strength, teach us to make war, and deliver us from the enemy. I ask You now to cause boldness to rise up in this child of Yours as they wage spiritual war for their harvest. Protect their precious seeds so Satan can't devour them. Cause their seeds sown into Your Kingdom to flourish and grow into a bountiful harvest in their own life and for Your eternal Kingdom. In Jesus' name. Amen.*

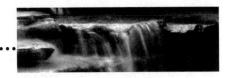

Chapter 17

Blessing Key: *Ten*

Wait Patiently for Your Harvest

Even when we've believed God, obeyed Him, and waited expectantly for Him to release His breakthroughs over our circumstances, sometimes our harvests may seem to be delayed. This can be frustrating, to say the least. Sometimes waiting is one of the toughest things in life to do.

Yet this experience has been faced by every man and woman of God throughout the ages. The psalmist wrote, *"I wait for the LORD, my soul waits, and in His word I do hope"* (Psalm 130:5). Perhaps you can relate to this as you wait for God to fulfill His promises in your life.

While many of us are surprised if we don't receive our harvest blessings immediately after we sow our seeds, the Bible is very clear that God's harvests often take time to develop: *"Let us not grow weary while doing good, for in due season we **shall reap** if we do not lose heart"* (Galatians 6:9).

This is very good news, isn't it? If we've been faithful to plant our seeds in faith, we *"SHALL REAP."* There's no doubt about it, because it's a promise from God.

However, we're *also* told that we'll receive harvest *"IN DUE SEASON"*—

not necessarily right away. And Paul warns us that we must not *"grow weary"* or *"lose heart"* while we are waiting. *The Message* translates this, *"At the right time we will harvest a good crop if we don't give up, or quit."*

You see, sometimes it's just a matter of *time* before we receive our harvest of God's blessings. In such cases, we must not grow impatient or stop sowing our seeds. The Lord's covenant **promises** involve a **process**, and the process simply requires time.

But there also can be a *different* reason as to why our harvest is delayed. Perhaps God hasn't released His blessings because He's waiting for us to obey Him in one or more areas of our lives. That's why it's always good to open our hearts to the Lord and make sure we've fully followed His instructions.

At times when Barbara and I have had to wait for a harvest from the seeds we've sown into God's Kingdom, it has given us an opportunity to prayerfully review some of the key principles the Lord has taught us about seed-sowing. Here are some examples:

- When you ask God for a HARVEST,
  He'll always ask you for a SEED.
- Your seed is WHAT God multiplies.
  Your faith and obedience is WHY He multiplies it.
- If you obey Him in doing the DIFFICULT,
  God will amaze you in doing the IMPOSSIBLE.

After you've ensured that your obedience is complete, you can wait expectantly, confident that your miracle harvest will come *"in due season."*

Seasons of Preparation

Often our impatience stems from an inability to recognize the "season" we are in. Ecclesiastes 3:1 says, *"To everything there is a season, a time for every purpose under heaven."*

God understands the seasons perfectly, of course, but it requires uncommon wisdom on our part to recognize His timing: *"A wise heart knows the proper time and procedure"* (Ecclesiastes 8:5 NASB).

For example, a wise farmer knows there are definite seasons of seedtime and harvest...

- ✤ Spring is when he sows his seeds.
- ✤ Summer is when he waits for his crops to grow.
- ✤ Autumn is when he reaps what he has sown.
- ✤ Winter is when it can be cold, dark, and dreary, and nothing seems to be happening, but in this difficult season the farmer prepares for the coming spring.

Do you see the beautiful rhythm here? Each of these seasons is vital. None is more important than another. But in order to maximize his eventual harvest, the farmer must understand and appreciate God's instructions for his current season.

It's the same in the spiritual world. Nothing stays the same. Change is inevitable. But we shouldn't be surprised if the seeds we've sown into God's Kingdom take time to sprout and grow into an uncommon harvest.

Let Your Roots Grow Deep

Depending on where you live in the world, the winter season can bring with it a cold and dreary waiting period. Winter's trees have lost their leaves, seemingly stripped of all life. Nothing seems to be growing from the frigid ground. No fruit. No beauty. And all you can do is wait and prepare for springtime.

But don't be fooled by the lack of progress. Beneath the snow and ice, life is happening. There's new growth and added strength—preparation for the bounty to come!

While spring and summer are times of upward growth for the trees, winter is a time of downward growth. Instead of their branches spreading up and out, filled with visible life and fruitfulness, their roots are growing strong and deep.

Friend, don't miss the vital lesson here: Without a winter season to bring needed rest, strength, and deepening, the tree wouldn't be able to *hold* all the blessings God will heap upon its branches in the spring! Instead, it would fall over in the first hard wind.

In the same way, God often uses the winter seasons of life to help you deepen your root system and your intimacy with Him. It's all part of His plan to make you a strong Christian, able to be His hands, feet, and voice in this needy world. And the end result is to make you a blessing, even as you are increasingly blessed by your Father in Heaven.

Let's be honest. As Believers, we tend to pray for relief from the winter seasons of life, not appreciating how they fulfill God's plan to deepen our roots. But I encourage you today to pause and *give thanks* to the Lord for strengthening your roots so you can bear more fruit for His Kingdom.

Surviving the Winter

My friend, I don't want to make light of any adversity you may be facing right now. If you are experiencing a winter season in your physical or spiritual health...your finances...your marriage or family...your emotions...or some other area of your life, my heart and prayers go out to you.

But please be assured of God's love for you, even in these dark days. Even if your entire world seems to be shaking, you serve a God who *cannot* be shaken (Hebrews 12:25-28). You can trust Him today, even amid your pain or confusion. Though life may seem like a whirlwind, you can build upon the firm foundation of God's Word (Matthew 7:24-27).

Remember: The more difficult the winter season, the deeper your roots can grow. These times of trial are part of God's refining process to grow your faith and show you how to lean on Him.

During the winter season, people may let you down at times. But not God. He will be ever faithful, for He assures you in *every* season of life,

"I will never leave you nor forsake you" (Hebrews 13:5).

In the dark days of winter, don't miss your opportunity to stretch your roots deeper. Let hope arise in your heart for a better day. Springtime will soon be at hand!

Instead of focusing on your circumstances during winter season, I urge you to...

- Focus on the Lord
- Worship Him
- Talk to Him
- Read His Word
- Listen to Him

Make this time of testing a chance to get to know the Lord more intimately than ever before. He wants nothing more—or less—than *all* of you.

Defy the Devil's Ds

All too often, we don't see the good of winter. Since the devil comes to *"steal, kill, and destroy"* (John 10:10), he will do everything he can to use this season to sow his...

- **D**oubt and **D**isbelief in your mind
- **D**epression and **D**iscouragement in your heart
- **D**efeat and **D**estruction in your harvest

Unless we hold fast to God's promises and the hope of our coming springtime, we will be vulnerable to these attacks. That's why it's so crucial to realize that the winter seasons are something God *allows* as part of His plan to strengthen us and bless us with greater fruitfulness in the end.

If you focus on your problems, the devil will undermine your faith and destroy your expectancy. Instead, you must look to God and remember His faithfulness, even when it's hard to see signs of it with your natural eyes.

Let the words of this beautiful Scripture passage comfort and strengthen you as you await your harvest of blessings from the Lord:

> *The LORD longs to be gracious to you; therefore he will rise up to show you compassion. For the LORD is a God of justice.* **Blessed are all who wait for him!**
>
> **He will also send you rain for the seed you sow in the ground,** *and the food that comes from the land will be* **rich and plentiful** (Isaiah 30:18, 23 NIV).

God promises to BLESS everyone who waits for Him. As you await His harvests, He promises to send you rain for the seeds you've sown into His Kingdom. And the result? A harvest of provision that is *"rich and plentiful."*

So wait on the Lord, dear friend. Even if you're in a winter season and can't seem to feel His presence...even if the future seems uncertain and springtime seems far away...even if you're still waiting to receive the promised harvest...know that God hasn't forgotten you. He loves you and wants what is best for you. And you can be sure He hasn't forgotten your faithful seeds sown into His Kingdom.

He is growing you up to be strong in faith, strong in grace, and strong in the knowledge that He is in control of your life. Know that it's often in our hardest winters that He holds us closest and shows us *"the width and length and depth and height"* of His love (Ephesians 3:18).

Springtime Is Coming!

Just as surely as winter comes, spring will follow. You WILL see His faithfulness as you walk in an obedient covenant relationship with Him. You WILL have a new beginning and reap His blessings in your life.

I'm confident your springtime will be filled with greater vision, stronger roots, and more answers to prayer than you've ever experienced before. I see a day ahead when you will experience a whole new level of contentment in your walk with the Lord.

Waiting may be painful and discouraging, but it's often the necessary season between sowing and reaping. Don't give up if you don't see immediate results. God frequently works behind the scenes in ways beyond your imagination or dreams.

And remember: Harvests don't spring up overnight in the natural world, and they don't spring up overnight in the spiritual world either. That's why the psalmist writes, *"I wait for the LORD, my soul waits, and in His word I do hope"* (Psalm 130:5).

So...

Continue trusting in the Lord.

Continue crying out to Him.

Continue believing His promises, because...

He is working *ALL* things together for your good (Romans 8:28). Your Heavenly Father *IS* faithful, and your harvest blessings are on the way!

Let me pray for you...

> *Heavenly Father, thank You for Your covenant with us that seed-time and harvest shall not cease. We're grateful for Your promise that we WILL reap Your harvests in due season if we don't lose heart. I ask You to please strengthen the faith of this child of Yours as they wait for their seeds to bear fruit. Let Your grace, mercy, strength, peace, and joy guard and protect their body, soul, and spirit as they await their breakthrough. May they be strong in You and deepen their roots during their winter season. We thank You in advance for the amazing springtime blessings you have in store for them. I pray this is Jesus' name. Amen.*

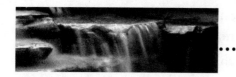

Chapter 18

BLESSING KEY: *Eleven*

CHANGE YOUR CHOICES, CHANGE YOUR LIFE

Are you tired of your circumstances? Are you frustrated by your inability to break free in some area of your life? Do you wish things could be different?

The truth of the matter is that you will never change what you tolerate—whatever you feel too tired, too overwhelmed, or too afraid to do something about. Even if you constantly complain about bad situations in your health, finances, or relationships, nothing will actually change by complaining alone.

But you also need to know that the things you *refuse* to tolerate—things you are willing to confront and do something about—CAN be changed. You don't have to remain stuck in your present circumstances, and it's how you *choose to react* to your situation that makes all the difference.

You see, you're the sum total of your choices—both good and bad. The decisions you make today will impact everything that happens in your life tomorrow. Actually, that's very good news, for if you want a better future, you can pave the way by your choices today.

God has given us the awesome, life-changing power of choice. Every day, we can choose between God's plans or the devil's...action or inaction...productivity or laziness...faith or fear...wisdom or foolishness... obedience or sin.

Years ago I heard these compelling words, which I'll never forget:

If you want to change your *future*, change your *choices*!

Not only do your choices affect your future here on earth, but they also determine where—and *how*—you will spend eternity. Even little changes and seemingly small choices can often bring huge rewards.

Yet too often, people simply blame their circumstances on someone else or on "fate." They absolve themselves of all responsibility for the negative situations they now find themselves in. But how can you move into God's land of More Than Enough if you refuse to acknowledge the vital role your decisions have in making that happen?

Life-Changing Choices

Perhaps you're familiar with the story of a young man named Daniel "Rudy" Ruettiger who made *positive choices* that brought about *powerful changes*. One of 14 children in a working-class family, Rudy was an average student and had no economic advantages.

Rudy had a dream of playing football for Notre Dame, but it hardly seemed realistic. At just at 5'7" and 165 pounds, he didn't have any special athletic ability or size, and no one thought he had a chance to fulfill his dream.

But the ability to choose is powerful.

Despite serious academic and financial obstacles, Rudy chose to begin at Holy Cross College. All the while, he chose to keep applying to Notre Dame, despite multiple rejections. And he chose to keep praying, working out, and studying hard.

When he finally was accepted for admission to Notre Dame, Rudy chose to walk on to the football scout team and give it his best. Even though he didn't get to play, he never gave up.

In the final game of his senior year, Rudy's lifelong dream finally became a reality: He played football for Notre Dame! After two plays and one tackle, he was carried off the field on his teammates' shoulders—one of only two players in Notre Dame football history to have been honored in this way.

Rudy's choices not only changed his own life, but they were a life-changing source of inspiration and motivation for his team, coaches, and family. All of his younger brothers went on to follow his example and attend college.

Friend, like Rudy, you may sometimes doubt that you "have what it takes" to succeed in achieving your dream. However, as Rudy's story demonstrates, the power to change your circumstances is in YOUR hands. Your *past* decisions have created your *current* circumstances, and your *current* decisions will create your *future* circumstances. It's really that simple.

So remember: The power of choice is life-changing, either for the better or for the worse. When you make choices that please the Lord, they will unlock His incomparable blessings and propel you into the land of More Than Enough.

Recovering from Poor Choices

In Luke 15:11-32, Jesus tells a story about another young man. Unlike Rudy, he chose poorly, and soon he was reaping the dire consequences of what he had sown. His story has become known as the Parable of the Prodigal Son.

This young man was tired of doing the right things, of working, and of being told what to do. He asked for his inheritance, then went off into the world, where he *"squandered his estate with loose living"* (Luke 15:13 NASB).

After the money was gone, he discovered that none of his so-called friends were interested in him anymore—and he was left with nobody who truly cared for him.

Before long the young man was starving and depressed—all because of his foolish choices. He ended up in a pigpen, an apt picture of how far he had fallen in life.

Remember what happened next? He finally came to his senses and made a life-changing choice to return home and ask his father to hire him as one of his workers. The prodigal's father, mirroring the love of our Heavenly Father, welcomed his son with open arms, lavishing great blessings on this previously wayward boy.

In many of our lives, there is a pivotal moment...a time of decision. And this certainly was true of the young man who found himself in a pigpen because of his poor choices.

The son could have kept on making the same bad choices. He could have complained about his circumstances and the way his former friends had abandoned him. But if he had made *that* choice, *he would have kept on starving*.

However, the prodigal wised up. He changed his choices and thus transformed his destiny. And although he probably expected to be reprimanded when he returned home, his father launched a great celebration instead.

My friend, I hope you have made good choices in the past, sowing seeds for a wonderful future. But if you've been more like this prodigal, making foolish decisions you now regret, today can begin your turnaround. Everything can begin to change for the better when you come to your senses and return home to the loving, merciful arms of your Heavenly Father.

More Than a Conqueror

Friend, the good news for you today is that you don't have to tolerate sin, sickness, fear, poverty, family strife, or any of the devil's other plans for you or your loved ones. God's plan is to give you overflowing life in the land of More Than Enough, through His Son, Jesus Christ.

In contrast, the devil wants you to believe you're a helpless victim, doomed to remain in the lands of Not Enough or Barely Enough. Instead of believing those lies, you must make a choice to look to God and His Word, trusting in His covenant promises to give you the breakthrough you need.

Of course, this doesn't mean you'll never be attacked by the enemy. Even *Jesus* faced Satan's attacks (Luke 4:1-13). But in Him, you can be *more than a conqueror* (Romans 8:37).

I love the example of King Hezekiah, who became very ill during his reign. In fact, one of God's prophets had informed the king that he was about to die.

Yet, did Hezekiah simply tolerate his death sentence? Did he allow himself to be overcome by fear, passively accepting death as his fate and God's will? No! Hezekiah wanted his situation to change...he wanted to LIVE.

King Hezekiah knew he needed a supernatural harvest. So he sowed seeds of humility before the Lord. He sowed seeds of heartfelt tears as he wept with a broken spirit and a contrite heart. He sowed seeds of fervent prayer, asking God to remember his faithfulness as he had served as a loyal king.

And God responded! Because of Hezekiah's seeds of humility, prayer, and tears, the Lord granted him an additional 15 years of life. You can read the entire story in 2 Kings 20, but I don't want you to miss this critical point: King Hezekiah refused to tolerate his apparent death sentence. Like him, *you* can refuse to tolerate whatever is going on in your life that is out of sync with God's plans and purposes for you.

This can be life-changing. Your turnaround can begin when you *choose to refuse* what you've been allowing. Nothing will cause your circumstances to change more quickly than that pivotal decision.

7 Steps in Your Turnaround

In order to exit the lands of Not Enough and Barely Enough, you will need to take seven positive steps toward a new beginning in your life:

1. **REFUSE** to tolerate the things in your life that you know are not from God.

2. **REPENT** for any sin that has contributed to your negative circumstances.

3. **REJECT** the fatigue, stress, or fear preventing you from making needed changes.

4. **RECORD** your specific goals for the needed changes in your life and how, with God's help, the changes will occur.

5. **RELY** on Him to replace old, negative habits with new, positive habits.

6. **REQUEST** God's mercy, strength, and courage to obey as you humble yourself before Him.

7. **REAP** His harvests as you expectantly sow seeds of your time, talent, and treasure into His Kingdom!

Remember: If you don't like the harvests you're reaping, then change the seeds you're sowing! If you want to consistently reap the things of the Spirit, then make sure you are consistently sowing seeds according to the Spirit.

The choice is yours, my friend, and I trust that you will choose wisely. God loves you so much. His heart's desire is that you love Him in return and choose to live in an unending, day-by-day covenant relationship with Him:

> *I call heaven and earth as witnesses today against you, that I have set before you life and death, **blessing and cursing**; therefore **choose life**, that both you and your descendants may live; that you may **love** the LORD your God, that you may **obey** His voice, and that you may **cling to Him**, for He is your life and the length*

*of your days; and that you may **dwell in the land which the** **Lord swore to your fathers**, to Abraham, Isaac, and Jacob, to give them* (Deuteronomy 30:19-20).

Notice that when you love the Lord, obey His voice, and cling to Him, you will be able to *"dwell in the LAND which the LORD swore to your fathers."* What "land" is that? It's the Promised Land...the land of More Than Enough.

Let me pray for you...

Heavenly Father, we praise You for giving us the power of choice. Thank You that we are not victims, but we are more than conquerors through Your Son, who loves us. I pray for this child of Yours, that You will lead them into more of the truth of Your Word. Reveal to them any poor choices that are impacting their current circumstances. And give them a desire to seek Your wisdom for every future choice they need to make to bring about the changes they seek in their circumstances. I pray this in Jesus' name. Amen.

Chapter 19

BLESSING KEY: *Twelve*

SOW CONTINUOUSLY, REAP CONTINUOUSLY

Every farmer knows that if he wants to reap a continuous harvest, he must continually sow seeds. A continuous cycle of sowing and reaping must be maintained in order to receive reliable harvests—and this is true in *both* the natural *AND* the spiritual realm.

The opposite is also true: Irregular sowing will inevitably result in irregular harvests. And, of course, if a person sows no seeds at all, they can't expect any harvest.

You see, sowing isn't a one-time thing, and neither is reaping. God can do amazing things for you when you're surrendered to Him, but He is looking for a life of daily obedience and consistent giving.

Think of it this way: You don't want to merely *visit* the land of More Than Enough, do you? No, you want to LIVE there! So in order to reap more than just sporadic harvests, it's crucial that you commit yourself to a lifestyle of regular sowing into God's Kingdom.

Never forget that a life filled with God's uncommon harvests begins with a habit of regularly sowing uncommon seeds. Your time, talent, and treasure—along with such things as praise, prayer, and obedience—are all seeds you can sow to honor God and reap the amazing harvests He has in store for you. The Lord wants to bless you and make you a blessing, and this is one of His primary mechanisms for making that happen.

It's impossible to fully unlock God's favor in your life without understanding and applying the incredible principle of seedtime and harvest. This powerful law goes clear back to the beginning of time, and Genesis 8:22 promises that it will *stay* in effect as long as the earth remains.

This is a principle throughout the Bible, from Genesis to Revelation. Paul wrote about it extensively in his second letter to the Corinthians:

> *He who sows sparingly will also reap sparingly, and he who sows bountifully will also reap bountifully. So let each one give as he purposes in his heart, not grudgingly or of necessity; for God loves a cheerful giver* (2 Corinthians 9:6-7).

The Message paraphrases this:

> *A stingy planter gets a stingy crop; a lavish planter gets a lavish crop...God loves it when the giver delights in the giving.*

Paul is saying here that if you don't like the quantity or quality of what you are reaping, then you need to change what you are sowing. You can't expect to reap an abundant harvest if you are sowing miserly seeds. And Paul adds that we should also do an attitude check when we sow into God's Kingdom, making sure that we are giving cheerfully rather than grudgingly.

Many people have the terrible misconception that they shouldn't *expect* anything when they sow their financial seeds. What a tragic error! Can you imagine any farmer who would plant seeds in the ground without any expectation of an eventual harvest? The Bible repeatedly says we should sow with a confident expectation of receiving a harvest of God's blessings in return.

Enriched in *Everything*

The Bible teaches that our Heavenly Father wants us to have an abundant harvest of His blessings—so much so that He even provides us with the *seeds!* The Apostle Paul writes about this incredible promise:

> *He who **supplies seed to the sower** and bread for food will supply and multiply your seed for sowing and increase the harvest of your righteousness; you will be **enriched in everything** for all liberality, which through us is producing thanksgiving to God* (2 Corinthians 9:10-11 NASB).

Notice that this passage doesn't say God provides seeds to *everyone*—it says He supplies those who are *sowers.* This means the best way to experience God's favor and His blessings is to set your heart on sowing seeds into His Kingdom. If you do, He will *first* supply you with seeds, and *then* He will provide you with a harvest from the seeds you sow.

And it's very important to realize that the promise in this scripture isn't limited to finances. It says that faithful sowers will be *"enriched in EVERYTHING."* Isn't that awesome? *Whatever* you are dealing with today—whether financial pressures, a broken relationship, an illness, an addiction, or problems on your job—God will miraculously step into your circumstances when you take a step of faith and sow your seed!

Remember: When you sow a seed into God's Kingdom, it doesn't leave your life. God takes the seed you've released from YOUR hand and then gives you wonderful harvests from HIS hand.

Jesus makes an incredible promise about this principle in Luke 6:38, *"Give, and it will be given to you. A good measure, pressed down, shaken together and running over, will be poured into your lap. For with the measure you use, it will be measured to you."*

This is wonderful news, isn't it? Not only does the Lord promise that you will personally receive a harvest from what you give, but He also says it will *overflow* and *run over*—blessing others as well.

Through the law of seedtime and harvest, you can have a life of overflowing abundance, my friend. And this means you will not just be enriched financially, but *"in everything."*

Perhaps you're a Believer who has sown seeds only sporadically...or maybe not at all. If so, I challenge you today to take a step of faith. Obey God. Make a new commitment to *continually* sow your uncommon seeds into good ground. And then wait on Him for His blessings and breakthroughs, because they will surely come.

Blessed in Times of Famine

Sometimes I meet people who have stopped sowing seeds because they are going through hard times—times of spiritual, emotional, or financial famine. While I'm sympathetic to their plight, I gently point out to them that it's *more important than ever* to sow seeds when they're going through difficult times.

We learn this principle from a fascinating story about Isaac, found in Genesis 26. He is just one of the many Biblical examples of how obedience, faithfulness, and expectant seed sowing will result in an outpouring of God's harvest blessings—even during times of famine and hardship.

> *There was a famine in the land...Then the LORD appeared to him [Isaac] and said: "Do not go down to Egypt; live in the land of which I shall tell you. Dwell in this land, and I will be with you and bless you; for to you and your descendants I give all these lands, and I will perform the oath which I swore to Abraham your father..."*
>
> *Then Isaac sowed in that land, and **reaped in the same year a hundredfold;** and **the LORD blessed him.** The man **began to prosper,** and **continued prospering** until he became **very prosperous*** (Genesis 26:1-14).

During a time of famine, God told Isaac not to go down to Egypt, where he would have had plenty of food and water for his household.

Instead, he was to remain in the land God had promised to his father Abraham.

When we read a reference to Egypt in the Bible, it refers not only to a physical, geographical location, but it also has a spiritual parallel to the world's system and way of doing things. In essence, God was commanding Isaac, "Don't look to the world or to natural things to provide for you during this time of famine. Look to Me!"

Imagine what it meant for Isaac to stay where there was a *"famine in the land."* He faced the terrifying prospect of terrible thirst...starvation... extreme lack...dire need...and a barren, unfruitful wasteland.

It was in the midst of this desperate situation that God told Isaac to remain in the Promised Land. With a future that looked so bleak, Isaac could have been tempted to doubt God's love and provision.

But Isaac's faith in God's love and faithfulness rose up within him, giving him the courage to obey the Lord and wait expectantly for His blessing—even in the midst of the famine. He knew his source was God, and God alone.

I've always wondered if Isaac's faith was bolstered by what had happened when he was a boy and his father Abraham took him up on Mount Moriah as a sacrifice to the Lord (Genesis 22). Was he recalling the terrible moment when his dad tied him to the altar in obedience to the divine command—only to have a ram provided by the Lord instead at the last moment? And was his faith still impacted by how his father's obedience that day had led to the revelation of God as *Jehovah-Jireh*— his faithful Provider?

While we may never really know what was going on in Isaac's mind and heart when he reached this critical crossroads in his life, we know what he DID during this famine:

Isaac sowed seeds!

Keep in mind that in a time of famine, seeds are very precious. They are the only hope for a future harvest, so you surely don't want to waste them. No one in their right mind normally plants seeds when there's no water, because seeds cannot grow without it.

I don't know about you, but many people are tempted to *hoard* their seeds during times of insecurity and lack. But not Isaac! He chose to trust God and sow seeds in the Promised Land even amid a terrible drought all around him.

And what happened when Isaac took a step of faith to sow seeds in the middle of this terrible drought? *God prospered him!*

Look again at what this passage says. In the very first year, Isaac reaped *"a hundredfold."* And notice that God didn't just bless him a *little bit* for his faithful sowing. We're told that he *"began to prosper, and continued prospering until he became very prosperous."* Wow. Wouldn't YOU like to have a life like that?

Making the World Jealous

The result of Isaac's obedience had another beautiful outcome as well: *"So the Philistines envied him"* (v. 14). Isn't that wonderful? Isaac was so blessed by God's favor that the watching world was *jealous* of him!

Paul cites the same principle in Romans 11:11, where he says God was blessing the Gentiles through the Gospel in order to make the Jews jealous enough to accept Jesus as their Messiah. That's what happens when the Lord takes you into the land of More Than Enough.

This principle reminds me of a scene I love in the movie "Butch Cassidy and the Sundance Kid." The townspeople asked about Butch and Sundance, "Who *are* those guys?!" You see, these two men stood out from the crowd (though not always in righteous ways!), and the surrounding bystanders couldn't help but take note.

The world should be asking a similar question when they see God's people today: "Who *are* those guys? How do I sign up to receive what they have?"

So even if you've never thought of God's favor as something you should pursue, remember Butch and Sundance. The world is watching. God wants to bless you in extraordinary ways, so you can make an extraordinary impact for His Kingdom.

The Seed of Kindness

Just as we must open our hands to the Lord, releasing our lives and possessions into His care, the Bible also repeatedly instructs us to open our hands to bless others. Instead of being miserly and trying to hang on to what we have, we're told to be generous, especially to the poor:

> *He who is kind to the poor lends to the LORD, and he will reward him for what he has done* (Proverbs 19:17 NIV).

> *If there is among you a poor man of your brethren, within any of the gates in your land which the LORD your God is giving you, you shall not harden your heart nor shut your hand from your poor brother, but you shall open your hand wide to him and willingly lend him sufficient for his need, whatever he needs... You shall surely give to him, and your heart should not be grieved when you give to him, because **for this thing the LORD your God will bless you in all your works and in all to which you put your hand*** (Deuteronomy 15:7-8, 10).

These are great promises, aren't they? If we are attentive to the needs of the poor, God says He will bless us in all our works and in everything we put our hands to do.

God blesses us so we can be a blessing to others (Genesis 12:2). And the more we set our hearts to bless God's Kingdom and people in need, the *more* He will bless us in return.

Some Christians, displaying either ignorance or false humility, like to say, "Oh, I never ask God to bless me. That would be selfish." Yet it's even MORE selfish for God's people to remain in poverty and financial lack, because then we'll have nothing to give to others.

Mother Teresa was renowned for her simple lifestyle and ministry to the poor. But few people realize that her generosity was only possible because she raised MILLIONS of dollars each year for her humanitarian outreaches!

The psalmist, likewise, boldly declares his need for God's blessing—not just for his *own* sake but so that the world may be blessed through his life:

> *God be merciful to us and* **bless us,**
>> *And cause His face to shine upon us, Selah*
> **That Your way may be known on earth,**
>> **Your salvation among all nations...**
>
> *God shall* **bless us,**
>> **And all the ends of the earth shall fear Him**
> (Psalm 67:1-2, 7).

The psalmist knew that salvation could only go out to the ends of the earth if God *first* blessed His people. So don't be afraid to ASK God to bless you! He wants to bless you so abundantly that people all over the world are touched by your example and generosity.

You don't have to twist God's arm to receive His blessings. He's *eager* to bless you—not just financially, but also in your health, relationships, and peace of mind. He knows that the more you prosper, the more people will observe His blessings and recognize what a great Heavenly Father He is.

Like any father, God wants to be proud of His kids. If your son was the championship quarterback in the Super Bowl, you would proudly tell your friends, "That's my boy!" In the same way, God wants us to live such victorious lives that the world will take notice.

Your Choice Today

Friend, I recognize that instead of living in the land of More Than Enough right now, you may still be struggling to leave the lands of Not Enough or Barely Enough. But with the right choices, today can be the day when your turnaround begins.

And although I don't know what kind of "famine" you may be experiencing in your life today, I *do* know you have a choice. You can look to yourself...the world...your job...your family...your friends...your church...or your government to be the source of your supply, or you can exercise your faith, obey God, sow uncommon seeds...and then wait with expectancy for God to step into the circumstances of your life with a breakthrough!

When you determine in your heart to be a faithful sower, *even* in times of famine, God will not allow you to run out of seed for your harvests. As you release the seeds in YOUR hands, He will *always* release the harvests in HIS hands.

However, God's harvest blessings only come as a result of faith-filled obedience. Regardless of whether you are living in time of famine or relative prosperity, He wants you to...

- Believe Him!
- Obey Him!
- Act in faith!
- Expect your harvest!

And never forget: Your Heavenly Father loves you and wants to meet your needs and bless you with a life of abundance. Like Isaac, you may even find that onlookers are *jealous* of how the Lord has blessed you.

Despite the numerous promises in Scripture, I still meet many people who are afraid to sow their seeds because they think that once a seed has left their hands, it has also left their life. This couldn't be further from the truth.

Your seeds *never* leave your life! Instead, God receives them and multiplies them back into your life in the form of the harvest you need. In the process, YOU are blessed, you can bless OTHERS, and GOD is glorified!

So go ahead and jump into the river of God's blessing. Choose to begin now to experience a life full of the blessings of seedtime and harvest. Get into the divine rhythm of giving and receiving, and then give and receive *some more*. Walk in a continual, loving, obedient covenant relationship with the Lord, and make these powerful principles a lifestyle. As you do, you will unlock God's blessings for YOUR life.

Remember: Faith + Obedience + Expectancy = God's Uncommon Harvests!

Let me pray for you...

Heavenly Father, thank You for Your deep and abiding love for us. We're grateful for all of the harvest blessings You want to pour out on our lives as we respond to You with faith, obedience, and expectancy. I ask You to please water the seeds sown faithfully by this child of Yours. Cause Your eternal covenant of seedtime and harvest to be a guiding truth by which they live. May they be blessed beyond their wildest dreams so that they may bless others and sow seeds to advance Your Kingdom. As they continually sow, may they reap Your supernatural harvests all the days of their life. I pray this in Jesus' name. Amen.

Part Three:

LIVING IN THE LAND OF MORE THAN ENOUGH

Chapter 20

WELCOME TO A NEW LAND

Although I've shared some powerful truths from God's Word about the great new life He wants you to have, there still are some crucial lessons to discuss. If you've been living in the land of Not Enough or Barely Enough a long time, it may take a while for you to fully adjust your thinking to the land of More Than Enough.

Remember how God miraculously delivered the Israelites from their slavery in Egypt? Even though they were able to leave Egypt in one day, it took 40 years to get Egypt out of *them*! They still thought like *slaves* at first, certainly not like a royal priesthood, sons and daughters of the King of Kings.

Like the Israelites, you will need God to renew your mind if you are to enjoy the full benefits of *your* Promised Land. Paul told the Romans about this vital process:

> *Offer your bodies as a living sacrifice, holy and pleasing to God—this is your true and proper worship. Do not conform to the pattern of this world, but be transformed by the renewing of your mind. Then you will be able to test and approve what God's will is—his good, pleasing and perfect will* (Romans 12:1-2 NIV).

Paul says that in light of God's sacrifice for you in sending His Son to die on the Cross, you should be willing to wholeheartedly give your life back to Him. Then the process of growth and transformation begins, when your mind is renewed by the Word of God.

To live successfully in the land of More Than Enough, you will need new ways to see God...yourself...your possessions...and other people. Put simply, you will need *"the mind of Christ"* (1 Corinthians 2:16, Philippians 2:5), for His ways are higher than your ways (Isaiah 55:8-9).

The Bible also is clear that if you're going to discover the full measure of God's covenant blessings, you must understand, accept, and practice the principle of seedtime and harvest. In fact, the power of seed-sowing is one of the clearest precepts in the Bible—first mentioned in the creation account (Genesis 1:11). And we're told in Genesis 8:22 that this principle of abundance will endure as long as the earth remains.

Don't be surprised, though, if you run into critics who say you're being selfish or materialistic to stand upon God's promises. "You shouldn't GIVE in order to GET!" they argue. However, if that happens, just remind the critics that Jesus Himself taught us, *"Give, and it will be given to you"* (Luke 6:38). I would rather stand with Jesus on this issue instead of the naysayers, wouldn't you?

So I hope you aren't procrastinating on this important key to a new level of abundance in your life. If you want to receive a future harvest of blessings, there's no better time than today to start planting seeds! The critics will pass away, but the law of seedtime and harvest will remain. And remember that the size and scope of your harvest will always be in proportion to your faith and the sacrificial seeds you sow into the good ground of God's Kingdom.

Stepping into a New Season

I've never been more convinced that God's heart is to give His people *"fruitful seasons"*—times when He blesses our lives with supernatural abundance: *"He did good and gave you rains from heaven and **fruitful seasons**, satisfying your hearts with food and gladness"* (Acts 14:17).

Yes, I've seen the reports on TV and in newspapers that the nation's economy is still going sideways. And I'm praying for those who have lost their jobs or homes.

Yet I'm also aware of this:

God can bless His covenant people *despite* the struggling economy!

The Bible gives this amazing promise to those who obey Him:

> *The LORD will open for you His good storehouse, the heavens, to give rain to your land in its season and to bless all the work of your hand* (Deuteronomy 28:12).

"But David," you may protest, "this hasn't been my experience. We're living in tough times, and I've really struggled the past few years."

If you're struggling, I understand. Barbara and I know what it's like to face challenges in our health, relationships, and finances. But we've learned that *God is faithful*, and we're praying for you to receive the breakthrough of blessings you need from Him.

Remember: Even many of the Bible's greatest heroes sometimes experienced times of testing or famine. Yet the Scriptures provide this incredible word of encouragement about prospering during tough economic times: ***"In the days of famine they will have abundance"*** (Psalm 37:19).

How is this kind of supernatural abundance possible? Let me share three powerful Scriptural principles for how you can enter into God's season of blessings, even when the world's economy is struggling:

1. **You can't buy a blessing, but you CAN sow your way out of a problem.**

    Remember that in Genesis 26, Isaac faced *"a famine in the land"* (v. 1). This truly was a difficult problem, so what did he do? Instead of becoming miserly and hoarding his resources, he determined to *sow more seeds*!

    Friend, God sees when you take steps of faith to sow of your time, talent, and treasure to impact lives for His Kingdom. And as He did for Isaac, He wants to bless *you* with a miraculous harvest of blessings...the envy of those around you!

Whether you need a financial breakthrough, a healing in your body, or the restoration of a relationship with a loved one, you can trust God by *sowing **SEEDS** to meet your **NEEDS**!*

2. **The sooner you plant your seed, the sooner you'll receive your harvest.**

Just as a farmer must be patient, the Bible teaches that we receive the fulfillment of God's promises through *"faith and patience"* (Hebrews 6:12).

Have you ever considered the fact that every kind of seed in nature has a different germination period? Radish seeds germinate in a week or less, lima bean seeds sprout in a week or two, but avocado seeds often don't germinate for six weeks.

In the same way, the seeds you sow into God's Kingdom may not always sprout as quickly as you would like. That's why the Bible encourages us, *"In **due season** we shall reap **if** we do not lose heart"* (Galatians 6:9).

Over the years, Barbara and I have received testimonies from *thousands* of Inspiration Partners who've received a miraculous season of blessings after planting their financial seeds. Sometimes their harvest was nearly instantaneous, but at other times they had to wait for weeks, months, or even years.

One thing is for sure, however: *Your seeds can't start to germinate until you've put them in the ground.* The seeds you plant in faith TODAY will prepare the way for your future harvest of supernatural blessings.

3. **God has placed special seasons on His calendar when He wants to bless His people in extraordinary ways.**

Although God is *always* pleased when we act in faith to sow financial seeds to honor Him and fulfill His work on earth, the Bible says there are "Appointed Times" when He wants us to bring Him *special* offerings, so He can bless us with *extraordinary* miracles.

Exodus 23 and Leviticus 23 designate the Feasts of Passover, Pentecost, and Tabernacles as these three "Appointed Times" or "Holy Convocations" that are special to God—a wonderful time to bring the Lord a special offering and believe Him for an awesome season of breakthroughs.

Barbara and I received this testimony from Crystal, an Inspiration Partner in Virginia who has sowed special offerings during these feasts of the Lord:

> *"Although I've always given tithes and offerings to the Lord, He began answering my prayers in amazing ways when I started sowing special financial seeds during His 'Appointed Time' feasts of Passover, Pentecost, and Tabernacles. He helped me pay off all my bills, and now I'm debt-free! Plus, He enabled me to buy an apartment building. I only had asked to be able to buy a home of my own, but God gave me an entire apartment building, large enough for me and other family members! Thank you for teaching me about these critical seasons for God's blessings and breakthroughs."*

Like Crystal, God wants YOU to experience special seasons of His blessing and favor. It's His will that you walk in health...receive His abundance...and recover everything the devil has stolen from you! His Word clearly teaches that you WILL experience His miraculous provision when you obey Him, understand His seasons of blessing, and step out in faith to sow your seeds into His Kingdom.

Whatever turnaround you need in your life—healing, deliverance, protection, a financial breakthrough, or a restored relationship—your special season of blessings can start TODAY!

Let me pray for you...

Heavenly Father, we give You praise for opening the door to a new season of prosperity and abundance in the life of this child of Yours. May they push through the doubts, the obstacles, and the critics to stand firmly on the covenant promises in Your Word. Thank You that we can experience abundant blessings even if we're surrounded by tough times in the world's economy! We trust You today with everything in our lives—our time, talent, and treasure. In Jesus' name. Amen.

Chapter 21

RELEASE GOD'S FAVOR THROUGH GENEROSITY

Over many years of walking with the Lord, my wife Barbara and I have repeatedly seen God's faithfulness in releasing His favor when we practice generosity. Even when it seems like everything else has failed to bring us the breakthrough we need, generosity often has unlocked God's favor and abundance in amazing ways.

Barbara and I have experienced, again and again, that you truly cannot out-give God. Not just in our lives, but in the lives of countless others, we've seen that those who live lives of radical generosity consistently experience an overflow of God's blessings. So if you're ready to be blessed like you've never been blessed before, generosity may well be the key you've been looking for.

Solomon tells us in Proverbs 11:25, *"A generous person will prosper; whoever refreshes others will be refreshed."* This is such a clear and powerful statement by the wisest man who ever lived. If we want to prosper, we must learn to live a life of generosity toward God's Kingdom and the needs of others.

Let's be honest: Generosity doesn't always come easily. But the first step is to recognize that *everything* we have is a gift from God. This means that we are merely stewards—trustees or managers—of the time, talent, and treasure we have received from the Lord (1 Chronicles 29:10-13).

Do you see how this perspective will change your life? It's not so hard to give if you recognize that it's not really *yours* in the first place. Also, realize that just as God has given you everything you already hold in your hands, you can receive even GREATER abundance when you faithfully *give* of what you have—regularly sowing seeds into God's Kingdom and the lives of others.

Jesus describes this principle in Luke 6:38 (NLT) when He says, *"Give, and you will receive. Your gift will return to you in full—pressed down, shaken together to make room for more, running over, and poured into your lap. The amount you give will determine the amount you get back."*

What a beautiful picture of the kind of overflowing abundance and favor our Heavenly Father wants to give to His children.

But it all starts with that important word: *"GIVE..."*

So remember: Favor is released from *God's* hands when we release something He has given us from OUR hands. And, Jesus says, *"The amount you GIVE will determine the amount you GET BACK."*

Often I meet people who act as if God's financial favor is a complete mystery to them. But it shouldn't really be a mystery if we have spent time studying the Scriptures. The Word of God is full of principles for us to follow in order to release His prosperity in our lives, and we neglect them at our peril.

Tithes and Offerings

One of the Lord's clear conditions for a life of financial blessing is to be faithful in sowing our tithes and offerings into His Kingdom. Although there are many other Biblical principles for unleashing God's financial favor, this is an indispensable starting point we can't afford to neglect.

Look at God's amazing promises, and warnings, in Malachi 3:8-12:

"Will a man rob God? Yet you have robbed Me! But you say, 'In what way have we robbed You?' In tithes and offerings. You are cursed with a curse, for you have robbed Me, even this whole nation.

Bring all the tithes into the storehouse, that there may be food in My house, and try Me now in this," says the LORD of hosts, "If I will not open for you the windows of heaven and pour out for you such blessing that there will not be room enough to receive it.

And I will rebuke the devourer for your sakes, so that he will not destroy the fruit of your ground, nor shall the vine fail to bear fruit for you in the field," says the LORD of hosts; "and all nations will call you blessed, for you will be a delightful land."

God's message here is packed with meaning that can change your life. First, He tells His people they've forfeited His blessings because of their failure to bring Him their tithes and offerings. This was no small matter, because God warns that they were *"cursed with a curse"* due to their unfaithfulness in this area.

But then the Lord shares an awesome picture of the abundant prosperity we can have when we are faithful and generous in our giving. In fact, He invites us to TEST Him in this promise!

For those who faithfully bring their tithes and special offerings into God's Kingdom storehouse, He promises to literally open *"the windows of heaven"* to pour out His blessings. Instead of giving us just barely enough to meet our needs, the Lord says He will pour out *"such blessing that there will not be room enough to receive it."*

This means God wants to give us blessings that *overflow*, with *more than enough* for our needs. As we're promised in Genesis 12:2, we'll not only be blessed in our own lives, but God will also give us enough to become a blessing to others.

This passage in Malachi 3 also says God will *"rebuke the devourer"* for our sakes. Do you see how significant this is? John 10:10 tells us that the devil is a thief who comes to steal, kill, and destroy God's blessings in our lives. John 10:10 also says Jesus wants to give us an abundant life, so we need to find out how we can overcome the *"thief"* along the way.

God provides the answer in Malachi 3. When we're faithful in our stewardship and walk in a covenant relationship with Him, *the Lord Himself* will rebuke the enemy and keep him from devouring our blessings! Isn't that good news?

Notice that Malachi 3:11 describes *"the fruit of your ground"* as part of God's favor toward those who obey Him in tithes and special offerings. In other words, He's promising an *abundant harvest*—but this promise only is relevant for those who've first been faithful to tithe and sow seeds into His Kingdom!

I pray today that you grasp this vital lesson in *permanently* leaving the land of Not Enough and the land of Barely Enough. When you put these principles of God's Word into action, He will give you overflowing abundance in the land of More Than Enough.

Give God What Belongs to Him

In many ways, it's a complete misunderstanding to say we're "giving God OUR tithes." In reality, our tithes *already belong to Him.*

I love the story about a man who took his young daughter to her first baseball game. Although she wasn't particularly interested in the game, she *loved* Skittles and was thrilled when a vendor approached their aisle.

The father gladly bought her some Skittles and then asked if she would share some with him. However, the little girl refused, saying, "No, Daddy, they're MINE!"

The girl's dad had purchased the Skittles in the first place, but now she claimed exclusive ownership over them. The father wasn't asking for much, but he expected his daughter to honor their relationship and acknowledge that he was the source of everything she had.

How sad that many of us act in the same way toward our Heavenly Father. It pains us to give tithes and offerings, even though we would have *nothing at all* without God's blessing.

The Bible repeatedly declares that God is the ultimate source of *everything* we have:

> *Every good thing given and every perfect gift is from above, coming down from the Father of lights* (James 1:17).

> *You shall remember the LORD your God, for it is He who is giving you power to make wealth, that He may confirm His covenant which He swore to your fathers, as it is this day* (Deuteronomy 8:18).

Verses like these are a great reminder that none of us is truly a "self-made" person, nor can we claim credit for any financial success we've achieved. Our material blessings have come *"from above,"* from our Heavenly Father. He has given us *"power to make wealth,"* for which we should be extremely grateful.

Because our blessings all have come from the Lord, He should get the glory for every good thing that appears in our lives. And in the end, everything goes *back* to Him:

> **From Him** and **through Him** and **to Him** are **all** things. To Him be the **glory** forever (Romans 11:36).

In light of such verses, isn't it silly for God's children to complain when a preacher encourages us to sow tithes and offerings into the Kingdom? I can hear it now: "Edith, I can't believe they're trying to get our money again!"

Somehow it has never dawned on some of us that it's not "our" money at all! Let me say it again: *Everything* comes from God and ultimately belongs to Him.

> *The earth is the **LORD'S**, and **all** it contains, the world, and those who dwell in it* (Psalm 24:1).

*Yours, O LORD, is the greatness and the power and the glory and the victory and the majesty, indeed **everything** that is in the heavens and the earth; **Yours** is the dominion, O LORD, and You exalt Yourself as head over all* (1 Chronicles 29:11).

I encourage you to take a few minutes and do this important little exercise:

- *First, look at your hands and clench them, making two fists.* This is the posture of those of us who hoard our blessings. However, there's a problem with this picture: If our hands are clenched to hold on to what we have, our hands won't be in a position to receive anything more. Even worse, we're likely to *squash* the things we hang on to if we squeeze them too tightly.
- *Now, unclench your fists, and hold your hands with palms facing upward.* You're no longer hanging on to anything, which may make you feel insecure or vulnerable at first. But realize this: When you open up your hands and release all you have to God, your hands are now in a position to receive back from Him an abundance of blessings—"More Than Enough"!

My friend, God is a *good* God, and He loves you beyond your ability to comprehend it. And because of the depth of His love for you, He wants to bless you with overflowing abundance.

I've never been more convinced that the Lord wants to transform your circumstances, your health, your relationships, your finances, and your emotions. He has a plan to get you unstuck and lead you into an amazing place of blessings—*"far more than you could ever imagine or guess or request in your wildest dreams!"* (Ephesians 3:20 MSG).

Chapter 22

REMEMBER THE FAITH CONNECTION

Throughout the Scriptures, faith and favor go hand in hand. In fact, the Bible says it's *impossible* to please God and fully live in His favor without trusting Him and exercising your faith (Hebrews 11:6). There's no other way to move from the land of Not Enough or Barely Enough to the land of More Than Enough.

What is faith? The Bible says, *"faith is the substance of things hoped for, the evidence of things not seen"* (Hebrews 11:1). Faith has *"substance"* and provides a confident assurance of God's unseen reality.

But if faith has substance...and if it has the confident assurance of God's promises, then why doesn't it always seem to work?

My friend, faith **does** always work—but not necessarily on our timetable or according to our wishes. God is ALWAYS faithful, and He wants us to trust Him with all our heart (Proverbs 3:5), even when we don't understand His purposes.

Often the problem is that we haven't truly *exercised* our faith. He is telling us to ACT UPON our faith, but we don't believe His promises enough to obey Him. Remember...

Faith will remain lifeless, useless, and powerless
until it's *exercised*!

I've heard some people say, "I don't have faith," or "I wish I had faith," or "I wish I had *more* faith." But Romans 12:3 tells us God has given *every* person *"the measure of faith."*

So it's not really a matter of having more or less faith. Faith is something you *already have*—but there's quite a difference between having something and actually *using* it. The Bible is full of stories about people who used their faith to see God move in their lives in miraculous ways.

Over and over again, the Bible speaks of faith:

"Your faith has made you whole" (Mark 5:34).

"According to your faith be it done unto you" (Mathew 9:29).

"Have faith in God" (Mark 11:22).

"He had the faith to be healed" (Acts 14:9).

"He did not waver in unbelief but grew strong in faith" (Romans 4:20).

"I live by the faith of the Son of God" (Galatians 2:20).

And these verses are just a small sample!

Our faith should not rest on the wisdom of men but in the power of God (1 Corinthians 2:5). It's not about what we know—in fact, it's not about *us* at all. It's about God's power and what *He* can do...if we release our faith.

And we must be clear about another factor: Sometimes we have to *wait* for our miracle. Hebrews 6:12 tells us God's promises are inherited through *"faith and PATIENCE."*

Just as a farmer must patiently sow seeds for a future harvest, we must refuse to give up if we have to wait awhile before we reap: *"Let's not get tired of doing what is good. At just the right time we will reap a harvest of blessing if we don't give up"* (Galatians 6:9 NLT). Notice the last line: *"We WILL reap a harvest of blessing,"* but then the writer adds, *"...if we don't give up."*

Don't give up, my friend! Your harvest is coming. Continue to believe that God will do what He says He will do!

Faith to Move Your Mountains

I often meet people who say they want to be an overcomer—yet they fall apart when God gives them any difficult circumstances to overcome! Somewhere they got the misconception that the Christian life is supposed to be easy and trouble-free. They desperately want to live in the land of More Than Enough, but they don't want to face any giants along the way.

Yet that's not what the Bible teaches. To the contrary, Jesus told us plainly: *"In this world you **will** have trouble."* Thankfully, He added: *"But take heart! I have **overcome** the world"* (John 16:33 NIV). Yes, He gives us the power to be overcomers—but He also gives us some things to overcome! His favor offers us victory, but it doesn't mean there won't be any battles.

Jesus compared the challenges of life to "mountains" standing in our way. And he gives us a startling promise about how we can move them:

> *"If you have faith as a mustard seed, you will say to this mountain, 'Move from here to there,' and it will move; and nothing will be impossible for you"* (Matthew 17:20).

Jesus said you can speak to the problems in your life and move them out of your way. He didn't say it would take *extraordinary* faith to do this. Even *"faith as a mustard seed"* can move away your mountains, and *"**nothing** will be impossible for you."*

Let this sink in for a moment. You don't have to remain victimized by your problems. You can go on the offensive and speak to them in faith by the authority you have as a child of God.

But I'm also intrigued that Jesus compares faith to a *"seed."* A seed is something you sow in faith, trusting that there will be a future harvest. The seed may be your money, your prayers, your time, or some other investment, but it's a key to moving your mountain.

But what should you do when your mountain *refuses* to move right away? You need to enter into God's presence and ask for His instructions...His battle strategy. As you enter His presence and put your eyes on Him, your faith gets stronger and He shows you where to sow your mustard seed of faith.

Psalm 97:5 tells us that our mountains can melt away in the presence of the Lord. In His awesome presence, sickness is healed...depression is lifted...addictions are overcome...poverty is defeated...and broken relationships are restored.

So if your mountain doesn't *move* when you speak to it, perhaps it will *melt* when you invite God's presence into your difficult circumstances. Either way, you don't have to cower in fear when a mountain stands in your way. No matter what trials and tribulations you may face, you can *"overwhelmingly conquer through Him who loved us"* (Romans 8:37 NASB).

Trusting God in Hard Times

It's one thing to say you're trusting God when you are on the mountaintop and everything seems to be going your way. But what happens when you're stuck in the valley and God's blessings seem hard to find? Will you trust Him *then*?

The Bible contains numerous stories of men and women of God who had their faith tested. They had to make a decision to trust and obey the Lord, even though their breakthrough seemed distant.

Perhaps you're going through a winter season in your life right now, and your faith is being tested. Maybe you don't see any way you can sow an uncommon financial seed into God's Kingdom. It just seems too difficult.

Yet I've discovered a surprising truth over the years: As hard as it may be, one of the surest ways to find victory in your winter season is to sow generous, sacrificial seeds. That may seem to run against all human logic, but it can be a powerful key to your new beginning in God's land of More Than Enough.

Remember: You are a walking warehouse of seeds. Everything you have is either *enough* (your harvest), or it's the seed you must sow in order to produce your *more-than-enough* harvest. I encourage you to follow Isaac's example and sow seeds into God's Kingdom and the lives of others even during your difficult seasons of life (Genesis 26:1-14).

This isn't just a nice theory for Barbara and me. It's something we've endeavored to practice throughout our years of walking with the Lord. When we've had a big need, we've sown a big seed. And we've seen God do amazing things in response to these simple acts of faith and obedience—not only in our own lives, but also in the lives of our friends and ministry partners.

No matter how dry and barren the fields may look around you, I'm fully confident of this: God will honor your faith...your obedience...and your expectancy. He encourages you to put His promises to the test and trust Him. He will give you a bountiful harvest from the seeds you sow into His Kingdom.

Smiling at Your Future

In recent years, I've met many Believers who have very dreary outlooks on their future. This is very sad, because God is clear about His plans for His children, *"plans to take care of you, not abandon you, plans to give you the future you hope for"* (Jeremiah 29:11 MSG).

What about *you*, my friend? When you think of the future, how do you feel? Concerned? Fearful? Anxious? Or filled with excitement and hope—confident you are living in the favor of God?

It breaks my heart to see so many Christians wringing their hands in fear over the world's economy...or wars...or terrorism—when God offers us keys to live in victory despite any outward circumstance around us!

Instead of hanging our heads in despair or waiting for a bailout from the government, we can model the amazing testimony of the faith-filled woman described in Proverbs 31:10-31:

*Strength and dignity are her clothing, and **she smiles at the future*** (v. 25).

Just as He did for this virtuous woman...

God wants to strengthen YOU,
so you can *SMILE* at your future!

When you have the Lord's favor and make Him your dwelling place amid life's storms and shakings, you can rest confidently in His provision, *smiling* instead of *fretting*! The Scriptures promise: *"A thousand may fall at your side, and ten thousand at your right hand; but it shall not come near you"* (Psalm 91:7).

This means looking to *God* as your Hope and Source—not to the resources or news headlines of the world.

This Proverbs 31 woman was confident in God's provision for her future, but that didn't mean she sat idly by, waiting for a supernatural harvest when she hadn't planted anything! We're told she had bought a field and *"plants a vineyard"* (Proverbs 31:16). And as God had blessed her, she was determined to be a blessing to others: *"She extends her hand to the poor, and she stretches out her hands to the needy"* (v. 20).

In the same way the Lord blessed this woman in Proverbs 31, He promises to bless *you* when you reach out to the least and the Lost (Proverbs 19:17). He will *pay you back* for every seed you've sown—giving you an abundant and overflowing harvest!

Let me pray for you...

> *Heavenly Father, thank You for being trustworthy and faithful in the life of this child of Yours. Give them mountain-moving faith as they claim Your covenant promises. Provide them with the courage to take bold steps of faith and reap an overflowing harvest of blessings. Thank You that Your plans for them are good, making it possible for them to smile at the future You've prepared for them. In Jesus' name. Amen.*

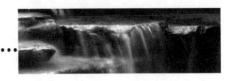

Chapter 23

HONOR THE LORD WITH YOUR BEST

One of the 10 Commandments tells us: *"Honor your father and your mother, that your days may be prolonged in the land which the LORD your God gives you"* (Exodus 20:12 NASB). This verse plainly says that if you honor your father and mother, you will live a long and blessed life. Paul notes in Ephesians 6:2-3 (NASB) that this is *"the first commandment with a promise."*

But there's another beautiful nugget contained in this promise as well. We're told that honor is a key to prolonging our days *"in the land which the LORD your God gives you."* What "land" is this referring to? The Promised Land, of course—God's land of More Than Enough.

This is an important and frequently overlooked aspect of walking in God's blessings. And the converse of this principle is also true: If you *dishonor* your father and mother, God's favor will be undermined, and your life will be shortened. You will find yourself hindered from leaving the lands of Not Enough and Barely Enough.

What About Honoring *God*?

If God put so much importance on honoring our *earthly* father and mother, just think how important it also is that we honor HIM as our Heavenly Father. In fact, honor is a powerful catalyst for God's favor in our lives. So what does it mean to truly *honor* the Lord?

Dictionaries define honor as "giving great respect," and there are 134 verses in the Bible that talk about honor. It's clearly an important topic to God, and many of the promises in His Word are directly related to our willingness to honor Him. Honor is another example of God's *"IF you do this...THEN I'll do that"* postulates.

You show honor to the Lord by obeying His commandments and doing what He asks. But you dishonor Him if you disobey Him. It's that simple.

If you honor the Lord, He will honor you. Honor will lead you to favor, and favor will open wide the gateway to His blessings in your life.

Do you want to release more of God's honor and favor in your life? Then the Bible's instruction is clear: *"Pride brings a person low, but the lowly in spirit gain honor"* (Proverbs 29:23 NIV). Whenever we truly humble ourselves before the Lord, He has promised to lift us up (1 Peter 5:6).

The Bible also teaches that we can honor God by bringing Him the *"firstfruits"* of our income: *"Honor the LORD with your possessions, and with the firstfruits of all your increase; so your barns will be filled with plenty, and your vats will overflow with new wine"* (Proverbs 3:9-10).

This is one of the most important verses in the Bible describing how to be blessed by God and receive His favor. The *"firstfruits"* principle means that when you get a paycheck, the first 10% belongs to the Lord, not just what's left over (*if* anything is left over). If you want to receive the full measure of His blessings, make sure to honor Him—and this begins with giving Him the first 10% of all you earn.

Are You Giving Your BEST?

When God sent us His Son to be our Savior, He was giving us His BEST. Paul writes, *"He who did not spare His own Son, but delivered Him up for us all, how shall He not with Him also freely give us all things?"*

(Romans 8:32). What an awesome God!

And since God so sacrificially gave us HIS best, shouldn't WE give Him OUR best as well? This seems simple enough, yet it's far too easy for many of us to drift into the tendency to give Him something much less than that—our *leftovers* instead of our best.

That is the same problem God confronted when the Israelites were giving Him second-rate offerings in the days of the prophet Malachi:

> *"A son honors his father, and a servant his master. If then I am the Father, **where is My honor?** And if I am a Master, **where is My reverence?"***
>
> *"...when **you offer the blind as a sacrifice**, is it not evil? And when **you offer the lame and sick**, is it not evil? Offer it then to your governor! Would he be pleased with you? Would he accept you favorably?" says the LORD of hosts.*
>
> *"**But now entreat God's favor**, that He may be gracious to us. While this is being done by your hands, **will He accept you favorably?"** says the LORD of hosts...*
>
> *"And **you bring the stolen, the lame, and the sick**; thus you bring an offering!*
> ***Should I accept this from your hand?"** says the LORD. "But cursed be the deceiver who has in his flock a male, and takes a vow, but **sacrifices to the Lord what is blemished—for I am a great King,"** says the LORD of hosts, and My name is to be feared among the nations"* (Malachi 1:6-9, 12-14).

What a chilling indictment against the people of God! Yet I'm afraid that we often have done much the same thing today. From time to time we each must examine our heart to see if we have been giving God our best or our leftovers.

This principle applies to every area of our lives and to every kind of seed God asks us to sow:

Our time – Do we give our best and most attentive time to the Lord or just a 30-second "Goodnight, Lord" prayer at the end of the day, when we're exhausted and ready to fall asleep?

Our talents – Are we using our talents and spiritual gifts effectively in furthering God's Kingdom?

Our service – Are we serving the Lord and other people wholeheartedly or grudgingly?

Our money – Do we give God the "firstfruits" of our income or just a portion—whatever is left over after we've spent most of our money elsewhere?

It's easy to deceive ourselves when answering these questions. Many of us do a lot of "sacrificing"—just as the Israelites did—yet we don't truly give the Lord our *best*. We give Him crumbs from our table, while withholding the things that are the most valuable.

Remember: As we see in the story of the widow's mite (Luke 21:1-3), the issue in God's eyes is not who gives the *most*, but who gives their *best*.

God wants you to experience His best, my friend, but that means you will have to give Him *your* best. The land of More Than Enough beckons you today, and the Lord has promised, *"If you consent and obey, you will eat the BEST of the land"* (Isaiah 1:19 NASB).

Take a few moments to pray and allow the Holy Spirit to search your heart. Let Him show you if you've dishonored God through blemished, second-rate offerings instead of your best.

Let me pray for you...

Heavenly Father, we want to honor You today with our best instead of our leftovers. I pray You will search the heart of this child of Yours and reveal any ways they have shortchanged You in their offerings and seeds. Stir their faith to sow generously in expectation of a bountiful harvest of blessings from Your loving hand. In Jesus' name. Amen.

Chapter 24

CHASED BY GOD'S BLESSINGS

One of the wonderful benefits of living in the land of More Than Enough is that you are literally *chased* by God's blessings. Inconceivable as it may sound to you, you don't have to be chased anymore by constant worries...overwhelming health problems...and bill collectors hounding you to pay your overdue accounts.

God has a better plan for your life!

Deuteronomy 28:1-14 paints a beautiful picture of some of the blessings you can expect when you're walking in God's favor and living in the land of More Than Enough. Not only does the Lord say you will *receive* these blessings if you obey Him, but He also says they will *"overtake you"* (v. 2). In other words, instead of you having to chase God's blessings, they will chase YOU!

And notice how all-inclusive God's blessings will be. You can experience His life-changing favor...

- In every place you go, whether in the city or in the country (v. 3).
- In the health of your body and the fruit of your labor (v. 4).
- In both your coming in and your going out (v. 6).
- In gaining victory over your enemies (v. 7).

- In being blessed in EVERYTHING you set your hand to (v. 8).
- In being established as a *"holy people"* to the Lord (v. 9).
- In a life of plenty, with God opening *"His good treasure"* to you (v. 11).
- In becoming *"the head and not the tail"* (v. 13).

But notice, once again, that there are *conditions* attached to this abundant favor. All of the blessings listed in Deuteronomy 28 are based on our response to God's invitation in verse 1: *"Now it shall come to pass, IF you diligently obey the voice of the LORD your God, to observe carefully all His commandments which I command you today..."*

Too often, when we read God's promises in Scripture, we overlook the conditions He includes in the context. If we expect to experience the kind of favor described in Deuteronomy 28, we must obey His voice and observe His commandments!

Take a few moments to pause and allow the Lord to speak to you. Is there some teaching in His Word that you've been ignoring? Have you hardened your heart to the voice of His Spirit in some way?

Make a fresh commitment to live a life that is pleasing to the Lord. Then get ready for a tidal wave of His blessings to overtake you!

How to Be Even *More* Blessed

Even after you've taken your first steps into the land of More Than Enough, you'll want to keep GROWING in your life of God's favor (Proverbs 4:18). So what if I told you there's a foolproof way to unleash an ever-increasing level of blessings in your life? Would you be interested in knowing the secret? I know you would!

A story in John 13:1-17 describes just such a secret. The setting is the Passover meal Jesus celebrated with His disciples shortly before His death. Jesus had stunned the disciples by removing His robe, wrapping a towel around His waist, and washing the feet of each disciple with a basin of water. It turned out that Jesus' example of humility and servanthood provided the disciples with a profound key for gaining more of God's favor:

> *After washing their feet, he put on his robe again and sat down and asked, "Do you understand what I was doing? You call me 'Teacher' and 'Lord,' and you are right, because that's what I am. And since I, your Lord and Teacher, have washed your feet, you ought to wash each other's feet. I have given you an example to follow. Do as I have done to you...Now that you know these things, God will bless you for doing them"* (vs. 12-17).

Did you catch the final line in this story—Jesus' statement in verse 17? He said, *"Now that you know these things, GOD WILL BLESS YOU for doing them."* After showing them an incredible example of what it means to be a servant—even to the extent of washing people's feet—Jesus said they should follow His example.

But a wonderful promise is included by Jesus: *"GOD **WILL BLESS** YOU."* You see, when you humble yourself and are willing to serve the Lord and other people, there's a *promise* attached. It's a promise of being blessed with more of God's favor and abundance.

Sadly, many people think they have to strive in their own strength to "get ahead" and climb the ladder of success. Their whole focus is on how they can *receive* more in life, so they're constantly trying to motivate other people to serve them and meet their needs.

Yet Jesus taught that this approach is backwards. Acts 20:35 quotes Him as explaining: ***"It is MORE blessed to give than to receive."***

So, if you want to be even *more* blessed, the pathway is clear: Humble yourself, and learn to be a servant. Set your focus on *giving* rather than receiving. When you do these things, you will be amazed at the new level of favor and blessings you'll experience.

Reversing Negative Circumstances

But what if you've found yourself in a deep pit of negative circumstances? How can God's favor help with *that*?

Every one of us has faced adverse circumstances at one time or another. Perhaps you are in the midst of a negative situation right now, and you're not really sure there's a way out.

Sometimes we encounter adverse circumstances because of bad decisions we've made in the past. Most of us have suffered at times in our health, finances, emotions, or relationships because of foolish choices that grieved the heart of God.

At other times, though, we face bewildering circumstances through no fault of our own. These are just the storms and winter seasons that are a part of life. Jesus taught that our loving Heavenly Father *"sends rain on the just and on the unjust"* (Matthew 5:45). In other words, some trials and tribulations are simply a part of the human condition, regardless of whether we are walking in God's favor or not.

Yet the Bible illustrates that faith and obedience often can *reverse* the negative circumstances that have undercut God's favor in your life. First Chronicles 21 tells the story of King David's sin in doing a census to determine the strength of his troops—even after he was warned that this would grieve the Lord.

God was angry at this and gave David the choice of three different consequences for his transgression. Each of these proposed judgments from God were severe, and David chose the option of three days of plague upon the nation. This plague was so harsh that in a short time 70,000 people died. But as the angel of the Lord was about to destroy the city of Jerusalem, the calamity was suddenly averted.

How was the severe tide of divine judgment turned? What can we learn from David's example in seeking God's mercy and finding the favor of the Lord once again?

God's angel tells David in verse 18 to *"build an altar to the LORD on the threshing floor of Ornan the Jebusite."* David obeys this word of instruction, and in verse 22 he says to Ornan, the owner of the threshing floor: *"Give me the site of this threshing floor, that I may build on it an altar to the LORD; for the **full price** you shall give it to me, that the plague may be restrained from the people."*

Although Ornan tells David he can have the land for free, the king refuses this generous offer. David's response may seem surprising to you, but look at his explanation in verse 24: *"No, but I will surely buy it for the **full price**; for I will not take what is yours for the LORD, or offer a burnt offering which **costs me nothing**."*

David's example should be a great lesson for us today. He refused to give an offering to the Lord that cost him nothing! True worship always will cost us something! Our offerings are seeds, and unless they're precious to us, they won't be precious to God either. He will never be pleased with our leftovers.

As David gave his sacrificial offering to the Lord, the plague suddenly stopped! We read in verse 27: *"The LORD commanded the angel, and he put his sword back in its sheath."*

Perhaps you're facing a "plague" of negative circumstances today. Your plague may not be the same kind David faced in 1 Chronicles 21, but perhaps it's a broken relationship, an illness, a problem with your children, an addiction, or a financial setback.

Regardless of the kind of attack you may be experiencing today, I encourage you to follow David's example and place your sacrificial offering on God's altar. As you take bold steps of faith and obedience, I'm convinced the Lord will restore His favor and blessings in your life. Your negative circumstances can be reversed, and you can take back everything the enemy has stolen from you!

Let me pray for you...

Heavenly Father, first we want to thank You for the blessings You've already given us. And now I pray You will give this child of Yours faith to see that You have even MORE blessings available as they put their full trust in You. Show them the steps they must take to be chased by Your blessings instead of being chased by problems and adversity. May You reverse every negative situation in their life today, enabling them to take back anything the devil has stolen from them. In Jesus' name. Amen.

Chapter 25

REVIEW THE CHECKLIST

Friend, I'm convinced your miracle harvest is closer than you think. But it all begins with the seeds in your hands.

Your seed is the **DOOR** to your future...the **EXIT** from your present... and the **BRIDGE** leading you out of the lands of Not Enough or Barely Enough into the land of More Than Enough!

So if you want to change your future, you have to change your choices and the seeds you sow. And remember...

- *Something* in your hand can create *anything* in your future.
- *Nothing* leaves Heaven until *something* leaves the earth.
- God won't ask you for something you *don't have*...
  but He WILL ask for something you *want to keep.*

**Just as your past decisions created
your current circumstances, your *current decisions*
will create your *future circumstances*!**

As this journey to the land of More Than Enough comes to a close, let me leave you with the checklist I shared earlier in the book, giving you the *7 vital steps* you need to reap your uncommon harvest:

1. Walk in a loving, obedient, faith-filled relationship with God.
2. Obey God's Word and the voice of His Holy Spirit.
3. Give each seed you sow a specific assignment for what you're asking God to do on your behalf.
4. Wrap your seeds with faith and expectancy.
5. Sow your uncommon seeds into good ground, continually and persistently.
6. Patiently wait to reap your harvest.
7. Thank God in advance, then honor Him with your testimony when you receive His uncommon harvests.

When you follow these steps, your turnaround will come. A bright new future is in your hands! You can step out in faith and obedience today, believing God for the supernatural breakthrough you need...

Your miracle harvest is on the way!

ABOUT THE AUTHOR

 David Cerullo is the Chairman and CEO of Inspiration Ministries located in Indian Land, South Carolina — a ministry dedicated to impacting people for Christ worldwide through media. David is a unique combination of Christian minister and corporate businessman. The son of international evangelist Morris Cerullo, David took a less traditional approach to ministry, graduating from Oral Roberts University with a degree in business administration and management. David and Barbara have been married for more than 35 years and have two adult children and five grandchildren.

We are Here for You!

Helping to Change Your World Through Prayer

Do you need someone to pray with you about a financial need…a physical healing…an addiction…a broken relationship…or your spiritual growth with the Lord?

Our prayer ministers at the International Prayer Center are here for you. Because of God's goodness and faithfulness, His ears are attentive to the prayers made in this place (2 Chronicles 6:40).

"God does tremendous things as we pray for our Inspiration Partners over the phone. It's such a joy to see people reaching out to touch the Lord through prayer, and in return, to see God embrace them and meet their needs." – TERESA, Prayer Minister

Every day, Souls are being saved, miracles are taking place, and people are being impacted for God's eternal Kingdom! We continually receive amazing testimonies like these from people whose lives have been touched by our faithful prayer ministers:

Debt cancelled… *"After you prayed with me, I received the cancellation of a $23,000 medical bill. The hospital called it an act of charity, but I say it was God!"* – MELVIN, New York

Son found… *"I had not heard from my son for five years, but I miraculously found him just two weeks after your prayer minister called!"* – Z.C., Missouri

Cancer gone… *"Thank you for standing with me in prayer and agreeing with me for my healing. The Lord has healed me of breast cancer!"* – NORMA, Michigan

Family restored… *"Thanks so much for your prayers. I've got my family back! The Lord gave me a great job, my wife was willing to take me back, and I've been clean from drugs and alcohol for almost a year. God is so good to us!"* – L.B., Colorado

This could be YOUR day for a miracle! Let our anointed ministry staff intercede with God on your behalf, praying the Prayer of Agreement for the breakthrough you need.

God Has Made Appointments To Bless YOU!

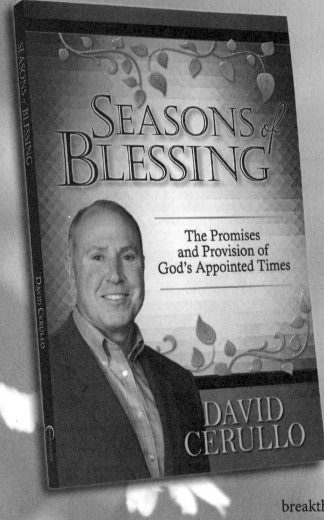

Are you ready to be blessed beyond your wildest dreams?

Whatever turnaround you need in your life — healing, deliverance, protection, a financial breakthrough, or a restored relationship — your special season of miracles can start with a step of faith TODAY!

Your Heavenly Father wants to step into the circumstances of your life with His supernatural breakthroughs. Learn about these special times when He offers to meet with you and bless you in extraordinary ways in David Cerullo's powerful new book filled with Biblical secrets that will transform your life!

"These are the appointed feasts of the LORD that you shall proclaim as holy convocations; they are My appointed feasts."

– Leviticus 23:2-3

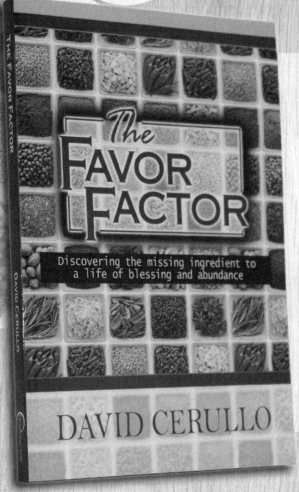

We Are Here for *You*

Visit us online today at inspiration.org!

- Daily Devotionals
- Incredible Testimonies
- Prayer Ministry
- Video Streaming

- Video teachings
  from David Cerullo
- Inspirational Tools
- Encouraging Articles

And more!

*This is just one more way we're blessing
and impacting people for Christ worldwide...
starting with you!*